REVELATION

REVELATION

Alun Ebenezer

 Books

EP BOOKS

EP Books (Evangelical Press), 1st Floor Venture House, 6 Silver
Court, Watchmead, Welwyn Garden City, UK, AL7 1TS

www.epbooks.org   admin@epbooks.org

EP Books are distributed in the USA by JPL Books, 3883 Linden Ave. S.E.,
Wyoming, MI 49548 order@jplbooks.com www.jplbooks.com

First published 2012

British Library Cataloguing in Publication Data available
ISBN 13: 978-0-85234-803-1

Scripture quotations are taken from:

CONTENTS

Second division

FOREWORD

I first came across Alun Ebenezer at a weekend away for Heath church in London many moons ago. What struck me was his relationship with the young people he was responsible for. I'd never seen any youth leader have such a connection with those around him. He managed it despite wearing a manky pair of rugby socks.

Gaining and maintaining that sort of respect is one thing but being able to give theological guidance is something else entirely. Mr Ebenezer is equally impressive when it comes to that as you'll discover as you read this book.

Alun can write a book ... and a very good one. Revelation is a tome that needs explaining — not only because it can be heavy going but because it's essential to our understanding of Christianity and the world we will live in. He has succeeded in making the last book of the Bible accessible to all.

Through studying the pages himself, and teaching it to others, he has managed to shed some fresh light on this amazing portion of

Scripture without feeling the need to use terms that belong in the eighteenth century.

Use it for your own Bible study, use it for a group, use it with your friends or family; but just use it. There is some serious meat in here which will keep you chewing on God's Word for some time and open your eyes to some of the truth behind the broad schemes of Scripture.

Dan Walker
BBC

INTRODUCTION

WHAT? HOW? WHO? WHERE? WHY?

WHAT?

What is Revelation?

Revelation is the last book in the Bible. It may appear at first to be a very difficult book to understand and full of puzzling symbols. But far from trying to confuse its readers, the purpose of Revelation was, and is, to comfort and give hope to people who trust in the Lord Jesus Christ. It is a letter (1:4, 11; 22:21), a prophecy (1:3; 22:10, 18-19) and a revelation (1:1).

As a letter, it was intended for specific people at a specific time in history. In the letter the writer wants to comfort the church in its struggle against the forces of evil. He wants them to know that God sees their tears (7:17; 21:4); and that their prayers are influential in world affairs (8:3-4). He wants them to know that the death of their fellow Christians was precious in his sight and that the final victory of Jesus Christ and his people is assured (15:2). He wants them to know that Christ lives and reigns for ever; that he governs the world in the interest of his church (5:7-8); that he is coming again to take his people to himself and live with them for ever (21:22) and that he is also with them now (1:12-20).

However, it isn't just a letter, and not just intended for Christians at the end of the first century. It is also a prophecy. God breathed out this letter and through it the writer interprets the events of history and the purposes of God in it. It isn't only meant for the first readers of the letter, but for Christians throughout history.

But primarily, this book is a revelation. God gives the writer visions to show us things we wouldn't otherwise know; things concerning God and his Son Jesus Christ, the Church, the world, judgement, the end of the world and Satan.

Even though the book should be taken as a whole, it can be divided into seven sections:

1. The Lord Jesus Christ in the midst of the church (chapters 1-3);
2. A throne and seven seals (chapters 4-7);
3. Seven trumpets (chapters 8-11);
4. The woman and the child persecuted by the dragon and his helpers (chapters 12-14);
5. Seven bowls (chapters 15-16);
6. The fall of Babylon (chapters 17-19);
7. The great consummation (chapters 20-22).

These seven main sections are parallel sections. They look at the same picture from different angles.

As well as the seven sections, there are two major divisions:

• Chapters 1-11 focus on the struggle among people, between believers and unbelievers. The world attacks the church but the church is avenged, protected and victorious.

- Chapters 12 - 22 reveal that the struggle on earth has a deeper background. It shows us why unbelievers hate believers so vehemently and what will happen at the end of the world. It takes us behind the scenes.

HOW?

How are we to understand the book of Revelation?

Revelation is a book full of symbols. The style of writing is called apocalyptic, which was a particular genre that was popular amongst Jews between 300 BC and AD 300. We are not to take these symbols literally but try to find out what they mean. Revelation is like a picture; and to understand it we need to look at the picture as a whole and not press the details too far. We need to think about the predominant idea and central meaning of the picture. As the book unfolds, the picture builds up and it becomes clearer and clearer.

There are four main methods of interpreting the book of Revelation. The first is to think of it as a book which was only relevant to the time when it was written, that is, to the persecuted church at the end of the first century. This method of interpretation would mean that the book has no real relevance to us today.

The second is to think of Revelation as a book which refers to events that will take place at the end of the world. This method of interpretation would mean that the book would have had nothing to say to the persecuted church in its present situation apart from saying that there is a hope at the end.

The third method of interpretation is to see the book of Revelation as a chart of world history from the first coming of Christ to the second coming of Christ. The seven churches in chapters 2 and 3 are not seven particular churches but seven ages of the church.

Some of the people who interpret Revelation in this way have found every conceivable historical character in it!

The fourth way of interpreting the book of Revelation is to view the book as dealing with principles of God's actions in history. But this method does not secure Revelation in a historical setting.

In order to have the best understanding of the book of Revelation, elements of all of these methods of interpretation should be adopted. Revelation was written to seven specific churches at a specific time in history to help them in their situation, but is also intended for the church throughout time. The book is all about the history of the world from the first coming to the second coming of Christ; however, it does not refer to specific events and people but rather applies principles of how we should interpret God's actions in history: i.e. the symbols in the book are not restricted to a particular event or disaster or war in history, but shed light on all events and disasters and wars in history.

Furthermore, in order to understand the book of Revelation, we have to know something of the contemporary background. The book is full of references to contemporary events and circumstances and so the symbols in Revelation should be interpreted in the light of conditions which existed when the book was written.

We must also put Revelation into the context of the rest of the Bible. It is important to let the Bible interpret the Bible. In other words, the other parts of the Bible will help us understand Revelation. There are parallel passages in other New Testament books, and Revelation is steeped in the thoughts and images of the Old Testament (for example, compare Revelation 13:1-10 with Daniel 7:2-8). Most importantly, there are parallel sections in Revelation itself: for example, Revelation 20 becomes clearer in the light of Revelation 12.

If we keep in mind all these principles of interpretation, our understanding of Revelation will be clearer.

WHO?

Who wrote Revelation?

The writer of Revelation was a man called John. He was one of Jesus' disciples. John had spent three years in close proximity with Jesus and was an eyewitness of all that Jesus said and did on earth. He heard his parables and saw his miracles; he listened to his sermons, observed his character and watched his life. No one knew Jesus better than he did. The night Jesus had his last supper with his disciples, John leaned on his chest (John 13:25). He stood by his cross and even entered his tomb. He saw him after he had risen from the dead and watched him ascend back up into heaven. He wrote one of the four Gospels with this aim, 'so that you may believe that Jesus is the Christ, the Son of God, and that by believing you may have life in his name' (John 20:31, ESV).

And now, on the Greek island of Patmos, one Sunday, this same Jesus appeared to John. In a loud voice he told him to 'Write what you see in a book...' (1:11, ESV). That book is Revelation.

However, the real author of the book of Revelation is God. It is 'The revelation of Jesus Christ, which God gave him... He made it known by sending his angel to his servant John, who bore witness to the word of God and to the testimony of Jesus Christ, even to all that he saw' (1:1-2). John only writes what is revealed to him by God. According to Plummer (*The Book of Revelation*, p.150), among the many noble sculptures by Thorwalsden at Copenhagen, there is one of the apostle John. His countenance is suffused with the serenity of heaven. He is actually looking up to heaven. His writing tablet is before him. In his hand is his pen. But the apostle's pen does not touch the tablet. He will not venture on a single word until it is given to him from above.

WHERE?

Where was Revelation going?

It was going to Christians scattered in the cities of Asia Minor at the end of the first century. It was probably written in AD 96 during the reign of the Roman Emperor Domitian. It was addressed to seven churches in Ephesus, Smyrna, Pergamum, Thyatira, Sardis, Philadelphia and Laodicea. These Christians were all facing difficulties and struggles of various kinds. Most were being bitterly persecuted. Their blood was being poured out (6:10; 16:6; 17:6; 19:2). Some were pining away in dingy dungeons, while others were about to be imprisoned (2:10). Some were suffering from hunger, thirst or famine (6:8; 7:16). Some of the Christians had been cast before wild beasts (6:8); many had been beheaded (20:4). False teachers and sects were troubling the church (2:2, 14, 20, 24). Emperor worship inspired false religion (13:7, 15; 17:18).

However, the destination of Revelation wasn't just the seven churches in Asia Minor. It was intended for people in every age.

WHY?

Why should I bother reading Revelation?

Because even though it was written almost two thousand years ago, this book is also for you. In fact, you and your life are on the pages of this book. The answer to all the problems you face and the questions you have are revealed in this book.

It is not easy being a young person in today's world. It can be a complex and complicated experience. As well as the issues some of you may face (abuse, family problems, money, bullying, sex, sexuality, drugs, alcohol, gang crime, relationships, peer pressure, education, lack of jobs, trying to be cool, wanting to be popular, the pressure to look perfect, depression, stress, nothing to look forward to), it is also an impressionable age when you start to think for yourself. You start asking questions like: Who am I? What is right and wrong? Is there a God? How did the universe come into being? Is there life after death? What is the point of it all? Why is there so much evil and suffering in the world? Why are there so many different religions?

It is not only difficult for young people. Maybe you are an older person reading this book. You feel the sheer emptiness of it all. You look back on a life full of shattered dreams and broken promises; of heartache and pain. You may be worried about the world your children or grandchildren will grow up in.

On top of all this, there's your own personal problem of a troubled conscience and guilt. The Bible calls this sin. You lie, boast, gossip, hate, get jealous, can be spiteful, swear, cheat, are selfish, and can be disrespectful to your parents. You hate being told what to do. You have dirty thoughts and you've done shameful things. You know what is right, but instead do what is wrong. Even though you don't like to think about these things, when you do, you know they are wrong, you feel ashamed, and know that one day you'll have to answer for them.

Revelation deals with all these issues. It reveals a God who made the universe, is in control of all the events of this world and will one day bring all things to justice when he brings this world to an end. It shows us the way things really are and what is really happening in the world. Revelation, according to Hendriksen, '...is true today; it was true yesterday; it will be true tomorrow, whether you live in Africa, Europe or America. It gives us the real philosophy of history. It indicates how we should interpret the news contained in our newspapers and the events which we study in history books' (*More Than Conquerors*, pp.34-35).

Maybe you are a young Christian and are struggling. You're being left out in school or college or university or in work and getting made fun of. You're finding it difficult to stand as a Christian and are tempted to give in to sin and give up the Christian life completely. You look at older Christians and the state of the church and find the whole thing confusing. Revelation is intended to help you. It explains why the world opposes true Christianity and that, even though Christians suffer persecution and hardship, God does hear their prayers and one day they will be victorious and enjoy eternal happiness with him. It reminds Christians that they are to be witnesses in the world and that Christ is in the midst of them showing them what they need to do to enjoy his felt presence. It encourages you and strengthens you to stand for Jesus Christ. Above all, at the centre of this revelation is a person. He is God's Son who died to save sinners. Through him we can have all our sins forgiven and personally know this awesome God.

FIRST DIVISION

SECTION 1

The Lord Jesus Christ

in the midst of the church

(Revelation 1 - 3)

1

ONE SUNDAY ON AN ISLAND CALLED PATMOS

Revelation 1:1-11

The events described in the book of Revelation took place one Sunday, probably in the year AD 96, on an island called Patmos, and were witnessed by a man called John (1:9-10).

So who was John, why was he in Patmos and what was so significant about this one Sunday in AD 96 that it needed to be recorded in a book for us to read today?

PATMOS

Patmos was an isolated, rocky, volcanic island in the Aegean Sea, off the coast of Asia Minor (Turkey). It was located about forty miles to the southwest of Miletus (Acts 20:15), which served as a harbour for Ephesus. It was ten miles long and six miles wide and consisted of hills that rose over 800 feet above sea level. During the first and second century AD, the Roman government banished people to Patmos. This was their way of getting rid of men they felt could have a harmful influence upon others.

JOHN

As we have seen in the introduction to this book, John knew and experienced that Jesus Christ was God and had come to this world to save everyone who would trust him. Knowing this, he was compelled to tell and write to people about these things. He wrote one of the four Gospels and three letters in the New Testament (1, 2 and 3 John). He was one of the leaders of the early church and an elder in the churches of Asia Minor (2 John 1; 3 John 1). The Romans persecuted anyone who acknowledged Jesus Christ, and not Caesar, as Lord. Therefore, John had to be exiled.

ONE SUNDAY IN AD 96

John was not the only one who was suffering, or who had suffered, for the Lord Jesus Christ. By now many Christians had been martyred and the rest of Jesus' twelve disciples had been killed. The churches in Asia Minor were suffering persecution, some to the point of death. Their leader was miles away from them. No doubt many were thinking of giving up, and some already had. Of this we can be sure: they and John were going through troubling times (1:9). But on this one Sunday in AD 96, John was given a revelation that would help and comfort not only Christians at that time, but Christians of all time; and give them a glorious hope for the future.

John is told to write down everything he saw (1:11, 19). The revelation was of Jesus Christ and had come from God (1:1) and whoever reads, hears and keeps what is in this book will be blessed (1:3). It is clear that the things John saw are important and that he had to write them in a book, known to us as Revelation.

BEFORE WE GO ANY FURTHER

The book opens by declaring that this is 'the revelation of Jesus Christ' (1:1). That this book is about Jesus Christ is what makes it so important. According to the author H. G. Wells, 'I am not a believer but I must confess as a historian that this penniless preacher from Nazareth is the very centre of history.' Napoleon said, 'I know men and I tell you that Jesus Christ was no mere man.'

So before we go any further and look at the actual revelation and what John saw, let me draw your attention to three important truths about Jesus Christ, whom this revelation is about. These truths are found in Revelation 1:4-8.

1. He is the Alpha and the Omega

In verse 8, the Lord Jesus Christ says of himself, 'I am the Alpha and the Omega.' Alpha is the first letter in the Greek alphabet and Omega is the last letter. The meaning is clear and is reaffirmed in verse 17, where the Lord Jesus says, 'I am the first and the last.' Jesus was at the very beginning of all things and he will be at the very end of all things.

The Alpha

The man Jesus was born roughly two thousand years ago to a young Hebrew girl. He was born in an insignificant town called Bethlehem, in a stable where animals were kept. His mother wrapped him in cloths and laid him in a trough. However, this humble beginning was not the real beginning of Jesus Christ. The baby born two thousand years ago in Bethlehem was in fact God. A key Christian teaching (though one which is impossible really to understand fully) is that there is only one God but this one

God is three persons — God the Father, God the Son and God the Holy Spirit. This is known as the Trinity. God the three in one has always existed and therefore Jesus has always been. He simply put on human flesh two thousand years ago and entered this world.

This fact answers one of the big questions in life: how did it all begin? In schools, colleges and universities, in newspapers, magazines, books and on television, it is almost taken for granted that in the beginning there was a big bang and from that big bang this universe came into being. Then over billions of years, life evolved. Almost everyone accepts this because it is claimed that scientists have proved or shown evolution to be true. However, on closer examination, this belief doesn't stand up too well. For any idea to be a credible scientific theory, it must be backed up by events, processes or properties that can be observed, tested and experimented on, to see whether the theory is right or wrong. The theory of evolution does not meet any of these criteria so it is impossible to prove that life began in this way. Nobel Prize winner Robert Millikan states (Blanchard, *Evolution: fact or fiction?*, p.7): 'The pathetic thing is that we have scientists who are trying to prove evolution, which no scientist can prove.'

To know what really happened and how this world really came into being, we need someone who was there. We need the Alpha, the first. The Bible says that this world did not come into being by a random, unplanned, accidental explosion, but by God. Genesis 1:1 says, 'In the beginning God created the heavens and the earth.'

According to Isaac Newton, arguably the greatest scientist of all time, this most beautiful system (the universe) could only proceed from the dominion of an intelligent and powerful Being. This powerful Being is the Lord Jesus Christ, the Alpha, the first, the one who is revealed to us in this book. In the opening verses of John's Gospel, John refers to the Lord Jesus Christ as the Word and says, 'In the beginning was the Word, and the Word was with God, and the Word was God. He was in the beginning with God. All things came into being through him, and apart from him nothing came into being that has come into being' (1:1-3, NASB).

The Omega

Not only is the Lord Jesus Christ the Alpha, he is also the Omega. Not only did he begin all things, he will also bring all things to an end. This is another fact that answers one of life's big questions. How will this world end?

Today people have different ideas about how the world will end. These include global warming or climate change, the earth being hit by an asteroid, nuclear war, and a reverse of the big bang where the universe collapses and becomes a big, black hole. Others try to predict when the world will end. Some believe that it will end following cataclysmic events in 2012. The Bible nowhere says *when* the world will end, but it clearly says *how* it will end and *who* will bring it to an end.

This world will end the way it began, by the Lord Jesus Christ. He was in the beginning and spoke a whole universe into being. Just over two thousand years ago he came into this world and became a man. At thirty-three he died on a cross, was buried and rose again. Forty days later many people saw him ascend back into heaven. As the people gazed up into the sky and watched him return to heaven, two angels asked them: 'Why do you stand looking up into the sky? This Jesus who has been taken up from you into heaven will come in just the same way as you have watched him go into heaven' (Acts 1:11, NASB). Here in Revelation 1:7, John says, 'Behold [take note!], he is coming with the clouds, and every eye will see him.' Jesus Christ is coming back! One day, no one knows when, he will bring all things to an end. The first time he came to this world, he

27

came quietly and humbly; the next time he comes, a trumpet will sound and everyone who has ever lived will be summoned to stand before him and be judged by him. A bigger question than how the world will end is really: are you ready for the world to end? Are you ready to stand before the one who will bring this world to an end? If you do not personally know and trust in Jesus Christ, the answer to that question is 'no'.

2. He released us from our sin by his blood

God is perfect and dazzlingly pure. In contrast, by nature all of us are sinners. Sin means missing the mark, falling short of God's perfect standard. It is a universal deformity of human nature. Sin is in our hearts, the pump out of which everything flows. We know we are sinners, then, by the way we think, speak and act. We lie, steal, hate, get jealous, are never satisfied but always want what others have got, have lustful thoughts, behave in shameful ways, use bad language, can be spiteful, lose our tempers, gossip, are cheeky and rude. Some of you reading this book might have even murdered, raped or messed up your lives with drink and drugs. All of these things show we are sinners.

However, none of the things listed above is the worst feature of sin. Most people no longer talk about sin any more. They talk about bad things. These are things which involve hurting others or are shameful. However, the real horror of sin isn't that it defiles me, messes up people's lives and destroys the fabric of society; the real horror of sin is that it is against God. It grieves and offends him.

The root of our sin is pride. We think to ourselves: 'Who is God to tell me what to do?' But in fact, he made us. He gave us every good gift we have, including the very breath we are drawing now! We owe him everything and yet don't think about him at all, and certainly don't love him as we should and as he commands us to.

You may still be thinking, so what? Well, whether you like it or not or believe it or not, one day you and I will stand before him and everything we've done will be revealed; nothing will be hidden from the eyes of a pure God. He is so pure that he cannot even look at sin. No sin whatsoever can enter heaven, but has to be punished eternally in hell.

To make matters even more desperate, there is nothing you or I can do to remove our sin and make ourselves right with God. We can't get rid of the past; nor can we stop ourselves sinning now. We need help; and the only one who can help us and deal with our sin is the one revealed to us in this book. John says in Revelation 1:5 (NASB) of all those who trust in Jesus Christ, that he 'released us from our sin by his blood'. But how did he do it?

Well, history records that outside the city wall of Jerusalem in a place called Calvary, on a Friday two thousand years ago, Jesus of Nazareth was crucified. The night before, he had been praying in a garden called Gethsemane. One of his disciples, Judas, betrayed him and a group of soldiers arrested him. He was tried by the Jewish council, known as the Sanhedrin, and then taken to be sentenced by Pontius Pilate, the Roman governor. He was laughed at, mocked, hit, spat at, and whipped thirty-nine times. A crown of thorns was squeezed on his head. Soldiers drove nails into his hands and feet and hung him on a cross to suffocate to death. Not only was he betrayed, but another of his disciples denied knowing him. Nearly everyone else abandoned him. A spear went into his side and water and blood flowed out. However, the worst part of all was when his own Father, the one he had been with from all eternity, turned his back on him. At that point, in absolute torment, he cried out, 'My God, My God, why have you forsaken me?' For three hours in the middle of the day there was complete darkness; after which the Lord Jesus Christ cried out, 'It is finished,' and bowed his head and died.

But what was really happening? Why did God forsake him? What did he finish? What was he doing on that cross?

The amazing, breathtaking news is that it was all for people like you and me. By dying on the cross he was releasing us from our sin by his blood. Instead of me paying the price for my sin eternally in hell, Jesus Christ was paying the price for me. He was taking my place, being my substitute. Instead of God directing his anger at me, on the cross, Jesus Christ was like a shield and turned that anger away from me. All my sin and guilt and shame were washed away by his blood. By trusting in his finished work on Golgotha, we can be declared just in the sight of God, completely pardoned for all our sin and declared righteous in God's sight. Every one of our sins forgiven and forgotten! The Bible uses the word 'justified', which basically means that my standing before God will be 'just as if I'd never sinned'.

But why would he do all of that? Why would he endure all that pain and torment? The only explanation is also found in Revelation 1:5, where John says the Lord Jesus 'loves us'! Think of it! The one who was in the beginning and will be at the end; the one who made this universe and will one day judge everyone who has ever lived, actually loves people like you and me so much that he was willing to die on a cross and shed his blood so that we can be released from our sin.

It is truly amazing. We don't deserve it; but the real secret is in Revelation 1:4 where John says, 'Grace to you'. Grace is undeserved favour; which means in essence that God is for us even though we are against him. This 'amazing grace', as John Newton put it, is absolutely free and available to all. However bad you are or have been; whatever secrets you are hiding, 'grace to you'! It is what makes Christianity different from all the other religions of this world.

One day a meeting took place in London where the topic of religion was being discussed. C. S. Lewis, the author of the Narnia stories, arrived at the meeting late. One of the men said to him, 'What makes Christianity different from all other religions?' 'That's easy,' Lewis responded. 'Grace!'

Every other religion teaches that to be right with God, you have to do something; do, do, do. Christianity says, 'Done'! Everything has been done for you. Trust in a finished work. Maybe you've been trying to save yourself. You've tried turning over a new leaf, giving up some bad habits, going to church, reading your Bible, even trying to pray, but none of it seems to be working. Like Lady Macbeth in Shakespeare's play, you have cried out in despair, 'Not all of Neptune's seas could wash away this guilt!' Well let me, as Staupitz urged Martin Luther, urge you to 'Look at the wounds of Jesus Christ, to the blood He has shed for you. Instead of torturing yourself on account of your sins, throw yourself into the Redeemer's arms' (Leahy, *Great Conversions*, p.15).

A story is told of a young Irish boy who went along to a mission to hear a famous evangelist preach about hell and sin and judgement and the need to be saved. The mission lasted a week and as the week went on the boy became more and more troubled. After the last meeting he went home and couldn't sleep. Over and over in his mind went the question: 'What must I do to be saved? What must I do?' The following morning he got up straight away and ran back to the field where the mission had been held. The organizers were taking the tents down and packing up. After looking frantically, the young boy finally found the evangelist. He said to him, 'Sir, what must I do to be saved? What must I do?' The evangelist said to him, 'You're too late, son. You're too late! In fact you're two thousand years too late. It's all been done for you. Trust in a finished work!'

Put your faith in the one who is revealed to you in this book, the Lord Jesus Christ. He can release you from your sin.

3. He is the Almighty

Not only is Jesus Christ the Alpha and Omega and the only one who can release us from our sin, he is also the Almighty. The people who would have read this letter for the first time needed to know this. They were in real tribulation and facing bitter persecution. John wanted them to know that the one who was persecuting them, Caesar, was under the control of the almighty Lord Jesus Christ. Even though Caesar and the Roman Empire were mighty, the Lord Jesus Christ is almighty. He has the whole world in his hand. He is the ruler of the kings of the earth (1:5), even Caesar. Kingdoms rise and fall at his command. According to Isaiah, 'The nations are like a drop from a bucket, and are regarded as a speck of dust on the scales; behold he lifts up the islands like fine dust' (Isaiah 40:15, NASB).

What was true when Revelation was written is still true today. God is still on the throne. He is still the master of the universe. The bully in your school, your teachers and lecturers, your boss, workmates, family, friends, neighbours, the rich and famous, presidents, prime ministers, kings and queens are all in his hand! He built every mountain and rolled out every sea. He put the sun and the moon in their place and named every star. When he was on earth, he healed the sick, gave sight to the blind, raised the dead and calmed the storm. His disciples exclaimed: 'Even the wind and the waves obey him!'(Mark 4:41, NIV). He is almighty, and he hasn't lost any of his ancient power.

He has power over everything, even death. Some of the first readers of this letter were about to die because of their faith in Jesus Christ; some people already had. John wants them to know that even this is under Christ's control. John refers to him as the 'firstborn of the dead' (1:5). He died and was laid in a tomb, but three days later rose again, conquering death once and for all. He was the firstborn of the dead. Everyone who trusts in him has the same victory over death and can face it without fear or dread. The apostle Paul, who wrote many of the books in the New Testament could say, 'O death, where is your sting? O grave, where is your victory?' (1 Corinthians 15:55). Christians can face death with confidence because Jesus Christ has conquered it.

Christians die well. Luther Rees, who was a famous preacher in Wales in the 1950s and 1960s, was dying and losing consciousness. His wife was holding his hand and his daughter-in-law said to him, 'Dad, you don't know who's holding your hand, do you?' 'Yes', he said, 'and he'll never let it go!'

The fact that Jesus Christ is almighty would have really encouraged the first-century Christians and it should really encourage us living in the twenty-first century.

It is even more wonderful when we realize that we have direct access to this almighty God. John refers to Christians in Revelation 1:6 as 'priests'. This means that all Christians can talk directly to God through the Lord Jesus Christ. No minister, or priest, or other human being is needed. The weakest, most feeble Christian can come before Almighty God in prayer. Maybe you're going through a tough time at the moment; struggling with temptation and battling with a particular sin; maybe you're being made fun of because you're a Christian and feel ready to give up. Pour out your soul to God, knowing he is almighty and hears and answers the prayers of everyone who trusts in him.

Furthermore, however tough the situation you are going through is, Jesus Christ has promised to give peace to all those who trust in him (Revelation 1:4).The peace Christ offers is not dependent on circumstances. Trust in Almighty God and, come what may, you'll know peace in your heart. In the words of J. C. Ryle, a Church of England minister in Victorian times, 'Peace sleeps best on the pillow of God's omnipotence [all-powerfulness].'

Probably the greatest encouragement to the first readers of this letter was that their present situation and condition would not be for ever. John says that this almighty Christ had made them to be 'a kingdom' (1:6). Christ ruled in their hearts and one day they would enjoy living and reigning with him in heaven. This world wasn't really their home.

You see, these people still live today; no longer in Asia Minor and no longer under the tyranny of Caesar, but in heaven with Jesus Christ, the Alpha and Omega, the one who released them from their sins: the Almighty.

2

ONE LIKE A SON OF MAN

Revelation 1:12-20

In Revelation 1:12-20 John records the vision he had of the Lord Jesus Christ. The fact that this vision comes at the beginning of the book is significant. According to Morris:

> *The Christians were a pitiably small group, persecuted by mighty foes. To all outward appearance their situation was hopeless. But it is only as Christ is seen for what he really is that anything else can be seen for what it really is. So for these persecuted ones it was important that first of all the glory and the majesty of the risen Lord be made clear*
>
> (*Revelation*, p.57).

In the West, Christians today are again a pitiably small group. In some places Christians are persecuted; in other places they are made fun of and left out of things. What Christians believe is seen as old-fashioned, out of date and ridiculous. Christianity goes against the trend of society and is seen as completely unimportant to the overwhelming majority of twenty-first-century people. It would appear that our hi-tech, cool, trendy age has outgrown God and the need of Jesus Christ to be its Saviour. So is Jesus Christ still relevant today? Are these things still important? Has Christianity had its day?

The answer to the first two questions is 'yes' and to the third one, 'no'! Jesus Christ has never been more relevant and these things have never been more important. Christianity will never have had its day. Lord Reith, the first Director General of the BBC, was once in a meeting with people discussing future programmes for the BBC. One of the men said that he believed Christianity was facing extinction and suggested making a series of programmes on the church to give it the send-off it deserved. Lord Reith stood up and said, 'Young man, the Church will stand at the grave of the BBC and every other corporation and organisation known to man!' When everything else has been burned up, the church of Jesus Christ will still be standing because she has a majestic and glorious Lord and Saviour.

So let's look at what John saw and keep it in our minds and hearts, encouraging ourselves in the sure knowledge that even though the church appears to be pitiable and pathetic, this is not the way things really are.

WHAT JOHN SAW (1:10-16)

It was the Lord's Day, Sunday, which is a special day for Christians. It is special because God made the world in six days and rested on the seventh. Furthermore, in the Old Testament, God gave his people ten laws that they must follow, called the Ten Commandments. The fourth commandment is to 'keep the Sabbath day holy'; which means one day of the week should be different from all the others, dedicated to God. Keeping this commandment is still important today because Jesus himself said it is. The Sabbath day was a

Saturday but changed to a Sunday, the Lord's Day, when Jesus rose from the dead.

Even though John is far from home and away from other Christians, he is careful to spend time worshipping God and drawing near to him. On this particular Sunday as he drew near to God, God drew near to him in a special way. John was 'in the Spirit'. God the Holy Spirit enabled John to hear a loud voice behind him like a trumpet. Whenever God had anything to declare to his people in the Old Testament, he gathered them together by sounding a trumpet (Exodus 19:16, 19; Leviticus 25:9; Isaiah 58:1, etc.). The voice John heard was like a trumpet. It called attention to the importance of what he was about to hear and see. This was something from heaven!

This sound like a trumpet came from behind John, so he turned around to see the voice that was speaking to him. When he did, he saw seven golden lampstands; and among the lampstands was 'one like a son of man'.

As has already been said, Revelation is a book of symbols which are intended to reveal important things to us. The seven golden lampstands John saw represented the seven churches the book of Revelation was first sent to. However, the number seven is an important number in the book of Revelation and denotes completeness. These lampstands not only represent the seven churches named in Revelation but all real churches throughout history, even churches today where you live, where the Bible is believed and Jesus Christ is preached. They're gold because they're precious.

The churches are pictured as lampstands because they are meant to give light. Churches today are meant to show the communities around them the truth: the truth about God, about heaven and hell, about sin and the need for forgiveness, and about the only

Saviour for sinners, Jesus Christ. Churches should show this in the way they live and the message they proclaim.

In the middle of these seven lampstands, John sees 'one like a son of man'. Jesus Christ isn't far away in heaven but, by his Spirit, he is among his people. He is in the middle of the churches. When John saw him he would have had a rush of memories because the one he saw was the man he had known so well. For three years he had walked the dusty streets of Palestine with him and seen him hungry, thirsty and tired. But even though John recognized him and he was 'like a son of man', Jesus was now in all his glory. While he was on earth, Jesus, the carpenter's son from Nazareth, concealed his glory and majesty. But now John sees him as he really is.

He sees him dressed in a robe reaching down to his feet and with a golden sash round his chest. His head and hair were white like wool, as white as snow, and his eyes were like blazing fire. His feet were like bronze glowing in a furnace, and his voice was like the sound of rushing waters. In his right hand he held seven stars and out of his mouth came a double-edged sword. His face was like the sun shining in all its brilliance (1:13-16).

What do these things mean? His hair shows us he is the 'ancient of days' (Daniel 7:9), pure, eternal and wise; his eyes can see everything, even inside you; his voice is commanding and powerful, like the deafening roar of many waters, and shows his sovereign authority over all the earth; his feet like bronze glowing in a furnace warn us of his approaching judgement; a long robe reaching down to the feet was, in those days, the mark of a person of distinction and shows the dignity and honour of the Lord Jesus Christ; the sash around his chest signifies that his saving work is finished. In those days a person would tuck his long robe into a belt round his waist while he worked. The fact that the belt is around his chest rather than his waist shows that his work is done. On the cross he accomplished all that is needed for sinners to be saved and made right with God. There is nothing more to do. His work is done.

Out of his mouth came a two-edged sword, which is the Word of God, what we know today as the Bible. For a sinner to look in the face of Jesus Christ would be impossible, like looking at the sun shining in all its brilliance!

The seven stars in his right hand are the 'angels of the seven churches' (1:20). In all probability these are the ministers of God appointed to serve him in the seven churches (2:1, 8, 12, 18; 3:1, 7, 14). The fact that they are in his right hand means they are protected by him. He has given them power and authority and he is always with them. This is true of the ministers, pastors and leaders of our churches today.

The image of the Lord Jesus Christ in all his glory coming to judge those who persecute his church and to comfort and purge his people should be taken as a whole. However, let me draw attention to some things from the vision.

Eyes like blazing fire

That the Lord Jesus Christ sees everything is both a frightening and comforting thought. It is frightening because he knows everything about us. Nothing you or I have ever done, thought or said has gone unnoticed. Every shameful secret we've hidden; every dirty thought we've had; every spiteful thing we've said; what we're like on our own; he has seen it all. This awesome, pure Son of God who is approaching in judgement knows it all. No wonder the Bible says that when Jesus returns men's hearts will fail them for fear (Luke 21:26). So how can it possibly be a comforting thought?

It is comforting because all the things he knows about us can be forgiven. The long robe down to his feet and golden sash around his chest shows that Jesus Christ has completed salvation for everyone who will trust in him. This salvation means that we can be saved from the judgement of God. Everything can be forgiven; even your deepest, most shameful secrets. I'm sure your friends and family, boyfriend or girlfriend, husband or wife, people you work with, go to school, college or university with, like you at the moment. But if they knew what you were really like they would probably change their opinion of you. If everything about you came to light, people would be so disgusted they might even want to spit in your face! There are certain things we would hate others to know about us.

According to legend, Sir Arthur Conan Doyle, who wrote the Sherlock Holmes stories, once sent an anonymous note to lots of famous people in Britain. The note simply said, 'You've been found out.' Many of them left the country! Can I tell you the same? You've been found out. But the one who has found you out is the same one who offers to remove all your guilt and forgive you for everything. There's nothing he doesn't know about you or might find out that will change his mind about you. He knows you better than you know yourself and yet still says, 'Come unto me.'

Head and hair white like wool, as white as snow

The fact that he is wise — symbolized by the white hair — should encourage us to trust him with all our hearts. He knows what is best for us. People today have so many things to worry and think about: the future; exams; relationships; money; mortgages; marriages; children; grandchildren. Why not bring all these cares and issues to the 'Ancient of days'? Trust him to guide you even when the way is tough and it doesn't make sense to you. He knows what is best.

Voice like the sound of many waters

But not only does he know what is best, he has the power to do what is best. What a combination! His voice is like the sound of 'many waters'. I once went on a rugby tour to Canada and sat by the Niagara Falls. They were so powerful and awesome; nothing could be heard over them. This is what the voice of the Son of Man is like. He has power over everything. The biggest issue or problem or decision you face; the people who taunt you or leave you out because you trust Jesus Christ; the situation you dread; they are all under the authority of his commanding voice.

WHAT JOHN DID (1:17-20)

When John saw Jesus Christ in all his glory, he fell on his face as though he was dead. This tells us a lot about true Christian worship. God is awesome; and when people come into his presence they tremble. Today, many church services are too relaxed and people approach God in a casual way. But this attitude and approach is alien to biblical Christianity.

But even though Jesus Christ is awesomely holy and majestic, he is also gracious and kind. He put his right hand on John and told him not to fear. He has good news for everyone who trusts in him: he was dead but is now alive for evermore; he holds the keys of death and hell in his hand.

This message needed to be told to the first readers of this letter who were being persecuted. We need to know it today. Jesus Christ is alive for evermore and everything is under his control! Trust him, love him, live for him! Everyone who opposes him will be judged and everyone who trusts in him will be saved. And he puts, as it were, his hand on us and tells us we need never be afraid to come to him.

3

'I KNOW'

Revelation 2 and 3

In Revelation chapters 2 and 3 we find seven letters addressed to seven particular churches in Asia Minor at the end of the first century. However, this book is also a prophecy and so these letters were not just for those particular churches but for all churches including our churches in the twenty-first century. The letters describe conditions which occur in every church in every age and have great relevance to us today.

The seven letters follow a similar pattern: Christ commends them for something (except Laodicea); he rebukes them for something (except Smyrna and Philadelphia); he gives them a warning; he gives them a promise.

To each one of the churches Christ says, 'I know'. He knows what they are going through; he knows their condition; he knows their difficulties; he knows their work; he knows their sin. Not only does he know, but he has a message that will reach down into their very situation and help them. It is a message of correction, comfort, warning and hope.

So, let's look at Christ's messages to the seven churches one by one and then apply them to our churches in the twenty-first century.

THE SEVEN CHURCHES

The church in Ephesus (2:1-7)

Ephesus was what we'd call today a 'sound' church. They believed all the right things and stood out against error. They opposed the teachings of the Nicolaitans, who taught that because Christians were no longer under the law but under grace they could behave however they wanted. In other words, because keeping the law, or trying to keep the law, didn't make them right with God, they didn't have to worry about the law at all. Against this error the Ephesians had held out strongly. The law is clearly set out in the Bible in the Ten Commandments, the preaching of the Old Testament prophets (God's messengers), the teaching of Jesus and the New Testament letters. Jesus summarized the law in Matthew 22:37-40: love the Lord your God with all your heart, and love your neighbour as yourself. Even though the law hasn't saved them, real Christians will want to keep God's law as they will want to please him.

But, the Ephesians had lost their first love. They didn't love Christ as they used to. The Lord Jesus Christ tells them to remember how they loved him when they first believed and get back to the way they used to be. They must repent: that is, turn away from their sins and all the other things in their lives that distract them from loving him, and love him as they used to. If they don't, before long the church at Ephesus will cease to exist. If they do, they will one day inherit paradise.

The church in Smyrna (2:8-11)

There are no words of condemnation for the church at Smyrna. They were going through a tough time. The Lord Jesus Christ says to them, 'I know your afflictions and your poverty' (NIV). The word 'affliction' here actually means serious trouble, the type of burden that crushes. Moreover, their poverty was extreme: they had nothing at all. Some were about to be put into prison, suffer persecution and even die (2:10).

But the Smyrneans are told not to be afraid but to remain faithful. If they do they will receive the 'crown of life'. The Lord Jesus also says to them that their suffering will be for ten days. This isn't to be taken literally, but means that it won't last for ever. One day it will be over and they will be victorious.

The church in Pergamum (2:12-17)

It was very hard to be a Christian at Pergamum. Pergamum was such a difficult place to live, that it is described as having the 'throne of Satan' there. It was the official centre of emperor worship in Asia and people faced death if they refused to acknowledge Caesar as Lord.

The Lord Jesus Christ reassures them that he knows how difficult it is for them. He knows everything about them, even where they live! He knows that despite the danger they face, they have not denied their faith. He knows that one of their members, Antipas, has already been killed. It hasn't gone unnoticed because everyone who trusts in Jesus Christ is special to him. He knows us all by name!

However, even though Christ commends them for their faithfulness, he rebukes them for embracing the teaching of Balaam. Balaam was a false prophet who advocated compromising Christianity with paganism. He maintained that because the heathen gods had no real existence, there was no harm in Christians attending idol-feasts and embracing temple prostitutes in order to obtain pagan approval. But these things clearly go against God's Word, and for this the Christians at Pergamum are rebuked.

If they listen to Christ's warning and take note, he will give them 'hidden manna' and a 'white stone with a new name written on it, known only to him who receives it' (2:17, NIV). This hidden manna means seeing Christ as he really is and spending eternity with him. The white stone is a 'ticket' that gets you admission to his heavenly banquet. On each of these stones is the name of the individual who has trusted in the Lord Jesus Christ. There are no group bookings for heaven, only individual reservations. Furthermore, the people in heaven continue to be individuals, with their own personalities; but these personalities will be perfected — glorified.

The church in Thyatira (2:18-29)

The church at Thyatira was warm. They loved the Lord Jesus Christ; but they lacked discernment. They tolerated the 'woman Jezebel'. This woman claimed to be a prophetess and led people to believe that immorality and sacrificial meals could not defile those in whom the Holy Spirit dwells.

Thyatira was a trading city and in the city were lots of trade guilds. To be successful in business you had to belong to one of these trade guilds. Each guild had its own god, and being a member of the guild implied that you worshipped its god. You were expected to attend the guild festivals and eat food, part of which had been offered to the gods. After the feast, the real immorality started! It was a difficult situation for a Christian. Either quit the guilds and lose status and position in society, even suffering hunger, want and persecution; or be part of the guilds and deny the Lord Jesus Christ. Jezebel taught that if you were a real Christian and had the Spirit of God inside you, you could attend these feasts and not be affected. You could have the best of both worlds.

Jesus Christ warns that those who follow the teaching of Jezebel will suffer. He had given them time to repent, but they refused; so judgement would come upon them. Some people think that because their sins are not punished immediately they will get away with them; but it is a dangerous thing to presume upon the patience of God. One day everyone will get what they deserve.

But those who remain faithful, and no doubt suffer in this world, will one day enter heaven and reign with Jesus Christ. They are told that Jesus will give them 'the morning star' (2:28). In Revelation 22:16, Jesus says that he is the bright morning star. He will give them himself.

The church in Sardis (3:1-6)

Sardis, the place and the church, was addicted to a life of ease. There was no threat of external opposition or any problem with internal heresy. The church was 'as peaceful as the grave' (Wilson, *Revelation*, p.41). The church had a name that it was alive, but it was in fact dead. Christ urges them to 'wake up' (3:2). To stimulate a desire for recovery they needed to think about the gospel, the good news about Jesus Christ.

Even though this church was in a critical state, there were still a few in Sardis who were alive and spiritually well. Jesus encourages them that their names are in the book of life and will never be removed.

The church in Philadelphia (3:7-13)

The Lord Jesus Christ has no words of blame for the church at Philadelphia. They had remained faithful despite the active hostility of the Jews. He promises them an open door to glory which no one can shut. They are going through difficult times at the moment but they will spend eternity in heaven and no one can prevent them from getting there.

The church in Laodicea (3:14-22)

The Lord Jesus Christ has no words of commendation for the church at Laodicea. They had absorbed the complacent spirit of an affluent society. They were totally ignorant of their real condition. They thought they were doing fine, that they were rich, but in fact they were 'pitiful, poor, blind and naked' (3:17, NIV). They were neither hot nor cold; completely indifferent towards Jesus Christ; totally complacent. Alarmingly, if you asked the Lord Jesus what he thought of the Laodiceans, he'd say, 'They make me sick' (3:16).

They were full of pride and deluded that they needed nothing. The Lord Jesus first tells them that this is far from the case; not only are they not rich, they are in fact desperately poor. But then he graciously tells this sickening church to come and buy from him and have all their needs supplied. Instead of trusting in themselves and their own goodness and self-sufficiency they must come and collapse in faith on Jesus Christ. If they do, he will make them well again.

THE CHURCH TODAY

If the Lord Jesus Christ wrote a letter to our churches today, what would he say? One thing is as sure as it was when he wrote to the seven churches at the end of the first century: 'He knows.'

Persecuted

There are some churches and Christians in the world today who are going through terrible persecution. According to a report in *Evangelical Times* (July 2010), Christians in Pakistan have been burned alive and seven professing Christians have been killed. Josefine Akhlas, from Lahore, said, 'There was nothing left of my house. It was totally destroyed. My husband was burnt alive.' Fifty-year-old Walter Masih lost his wife Pervan and daughter Asia when a mob poured chemicals into his house and set it ablaze. He said, 'My daughter was caught in the fire and did not come out. She was six months pregnant. We are very scared.'

In Java, Indonesia, Christians have been ordered to stop holding services and have suffered violence and loss at the hands of their Muslim neighbours.

To these Christians in Pakistan and Indonesia, the Lord Jesus Christ says, 'I know.' He knows exactly what they are going through. At this moment Pervan and Asia are with him; they've received the 'crown of life'. To Josefine and Walter and all their fellow Christians, he says that it will only be like this for 'ten days'. One day soon it will all be over and they too will receive the crown of life.

Maybe you have not had to suffer such persecution, or ever will; but perhaps you are getting picked on by your friends for being a Christian. Or maybe you are the only one in your family who trusts in Jesus Christ, and you are having a really hard time at home. Again, the Lord Jesus Christ knows. He knows where you live. He has been in your home. He knows the college or school you attend. Wherever you are, by his Spirit, he's there too. Whatever situation you are in, there are always two of you; you and the one whose voice is like 'the sound of many waters'.

Worldly

However, I imagine most of you reading this book are not suffering any kind of persecution, but rather you've been completely influenced by society. We are somehow under the impression that we can have the best of both worlds. We attend church on a Sunday but go to night clubs and pubs on a Friday and Saturday. We watch the same television programmes and films as everyone else because it doesn't really affect us, we say. We are Christians on Sunday, and maybe on camps and conferences in the summer; but then we get involved with all kinds of immorality when we're not with our 'church mates'. We want to get on in our careers; and if that means working on a Sunday, telling the odd lie, or not missing out on staff socials, then so be it. But Christ knows, and his message to us is: repent! Turn away from this worldliness; stop living double lives. 'How long will you waver between two opinions? If the LORD is God, follow him' (1 Kings 18:21, NIV).

Sound

I'm sure that many of you reading this book attend 'sound' churches. However, maybe some of you are not sure what a 'sound' church is. A sound church is a church that:

- believes and teaches the Bible as the Word of God from cover to cover;
- believes that only through faith in Christ alone can a person be right with God;
- proclaims the gospel;
- believes preaching is the way ordained by God to communicate the gospel;
- is reverent in worship;
- sees the necessity of prayer;
- has a love for the lost;
- has love for each other.

It is important to go to a good, sound church; to be doctrinally correct and to stand against error. For this the Ephesians were commended. We are meant to judge everything that is taught and takes place in our churches against the Word of God, the Bible. We are to be discerning and be careful that heresy (false teaching) doesn't come into our churches. The church at Thyatira was rebuked because they lacked discernment. Every book you read, every sermon you listen to, every service you attend and every event that takes place in, or organized by, your church, should be measured against the Word of God. To be sound and to be discerning is so important.

Loving

However, important though it is, it is not enough. There are many sound, correct churches around today which have no real love for Jesus Christ. It is as if they've dried up and gone cold. The love they once had has been lost. Above all else, Christ wants us to love him. All the other things we do are because we love him.

But how can we know we love him? Well, do we delight in reading the Bible? Do we spend time in prayer? Do we love other Christians? Do we have a burden that so many of our friends, family, classmates, college friends and work colleagues are on their way to a lost eternity? Do we keep his commandments because we want to please him? These are all signs that we love him.

If you did love him like this but you no longer do, remember what it used to be like. Remember what it was like when you first trusted him, and repent and seek him as you did at first. Imagine a husband and wife. They used to be so much in love but now their marriage has gone stale. They don't spend much time together because they are so busy and everything else has taken over. They are tired and don't make much effort with one another. To rekindle their love they go back to where they first met; they spend time together and fall in love again; they start to make time for each other once more. If we've lost our love for Christ then we have to do something similar. We are to 'survey the wondrous cross on which the prince of glory died'. Meditate, that is, think deeply, on his love, his grace and his mercy.

Indifferent

But maybe the worst state to be in is the one where we are lukewarm; totally indifferent and apathetic; thinking that everything is okay and we're doing fine; not relying on God at all. We need to realize our condition and our total dependence on the Lord Jesus Christ. We must come to him humbly and say in the words of the hymn-writer Augustus Toplady:

> Nothing in my hand I bring,
> Simply to Thy cross I cling;
> Naked, come to Thee for dress;
> Helpless, look to Thee for grace;
> Foul, I to the fountain fly;
> Wash me, Saviour, or I die.

The good news is that whatever our condition, Christ stands at the door of our hearts and knocks. If we hear his voice and open the door, he will come in and eat with us (3:20). If we seek Christ with all of our hearts, he will draw near to us and heal us of all our sins and strengthen us, however poor our condition is. He'll meet us where we are!

Don't you long for that? Don't you long to really know Jesus Christ? Don't you long for his felt presence?

Going out for food with friends or having people round for a meal is a big, enjoyable occasion. It's a time to relax, eat good food and spend time with friends. Jesus promises that if we open the door of our hearts to him he will come and eat with us, that is, have close communion and fellowship with us.

According to Tozer, 'a loving personality dominates the Bible …
men can know God with at least the same degree of immediacy as
they know any other person or thing that comes within the field
of their experience' (*The Pursuit of God*, p.50). The apostle Paul's
longing was 'that I may know him' (Philippians 3:10, NKJV). He
wanted to get to know Christ more and more intimately.

If we seek him with all our hearts we will know him intimately. We
do this by reading and meditating on the Bible; praying; attending
church and listening to preaching; singing hymns; attending the
prayer meeting; being obedient; loving other Christians; loving
those who are not saved; having a forgiving spirit; being thankful;
coming to the Lord's Table.

THE CHURCH ONE DAY

In chapters 2 and 3 we have a description of what the church was
like at the end of the first century and also what it is like today
— doctrinally compromised, morally lax, spiritually dying,
evangelistically ineffective, suffering and persecuted.

However, it will not always be like this. In Revelation 21 and 22
we have a description of what the church will be like one day:
glorious, triumphant, happy and perfect. Through the remainder
of this book we will find out how all this will happen. For now, be
strong, keep trusting, resist temptation, keep vigilant and love him
with all your heart.

SECTION 2

A throne and seven seals

(Revelation 4 - 7)

4

BEHOLD A THRONE

Revelation 4

As we have seen, the seven churches the book of Revelation was first sent to were mostly in a pitiable state. They were struggling with the pressure of the outside world and faced economic oppression, social exclusion and even the threat of physical violence because they were Christians.

In some parts of the world today Christians still face real persecution. In other parts of the world they are a pitiable small group. They are made fun of and left out of things. What Christians believe is seen as old-fashioned, out of date and even ridiculous. Christianity goes against the trend of society and is seen as completely unimportant to the overwhelming majority of twenty-first-century people. It would appear that our hi-tech, cool, trendy age has outgrown Christianity.

Maybe you feel that the Christian life is just too difficult. You don't want to be socially excluded and the pressure of the world is too much.

If this world was all there was and there was no God and no one in control of history, then this would be an understandable way to feel. After all, what would be the point? However, in Revelation 4 a door is open in heaven. John is taken to the throne-room of the whole universe and sees things from a whole new perspective. He sees things as they really are; from the vantage point of heaven. Only from here can things be seen in their true perspective. He realizes that this throne is the centre of the universe; everyone is in submission to this throne; everything is working for the good of those who trust in the one who sits on this throne.

So let's do what John tells us to and 'behold' the throne.

ON THE THRONE

John saw that the one sitting on the throne was like a jasper stone and sardius in appearance (4:3). The jasper stone portrays the dazzling brightness of God's holiness, whereas the blood-red sardius illustrates his avenging judgement.

Holy

God is holy. This means he is distinct from all his creatures and is exalted above them in immeasurable majesty. It is impossible for a human being to comprehend the holiness of God. It creates within us a sense of awe and absolute nothingness. The holiness of God also means he is completely separate from evil and sin. Because God is holy he cannot have any communion with sin (Job 34:10; Habakkuk 1:13). He is perfect. When a man or a woman is confronted with the holiness of God they have an overwhelming sense of impurity and an awareness of sin (Isaiah 6:5). We are totally unworthy to stand in the presence of this holy God.

Judgement

John saw that on the throne which rules the whole universe is a God who is holy and who will one day come to judge the world. Even though at the moment evil seems rampant and people who have no thought for God or interest in him seem so powerful, John's vision of heaven shows that these appearances are deceptive and that earthly power is transient. Real power is with God, who is holy and will judge all people one day. This judgement is certain. He has a fixed day on which he will judge the world in righteousness (Acts 17:31). All humans of all ages will be judged. It is unimaginable but human imagination is no measure of what a sovereign God can and will do. Everyone will get what they deserve (Romans 2:6).

FROM THE THRONE

John saw flashes of lightning and heard sounds and peals of thunder coming from the throne (4:5). These lightnings and voices and thunders express the dreadful power and majesty of God.

His majesty combines his strength, light, exaltation, greatness, magnificence and dignity. By his strength God spoke a whole universe into being (Genesis 1:1).

It is very hard to comprehend the power of God but think of it like this:

> *We live on a planet called Earth that orbits a star called the sun at a distance of some 93 million miles. Our sun belongs to a galaxy called the Milky Way which contains about 100,000 million other stars... Our galaxy is not alone in the universe but is just one of 100,000 million other galaxies. And God made all this — out of nothing — by simply speaking!*
> (Christofides, *The Life Sentence*, p.11).

Or

Imagine you got into a fast car and wanted to travel to the sun on the newly opened interstellar highway. Let us imagine it is a very fast car and that you travel at 150 miles per hour and that you never stop for fuel, food or rest. At 150 miles per hour, 24 hours a day, 365 days a year, it would take you 70 years to reach the sun! Having been there a while, you decide to head off for the next nearest star, Alpha Centauri, *some four light years away. You travel at the same speed of 150 miles per hour and 15 million years later you are approaching the outskirts of* Alpha Centauri! *And God made all this and beyond*

(*ibid*, p.13).

He is also light and in him is no darkness at all (1 John 1:5); he created light (Genesis 1:3) and is clothed in light (Psalm 104:2). His dreadful, awesome power is such that he can bring to pass whatever he pleases! We should be still and know that he is God. He will be exalted among the nations and exalted in the earth (Psalm 46:10). 'Great is the Lord and highly to be praised; and his greatness is unsearchable' (Psalm 145:3, NASB).

Today we have tried to bring God down to our level and made Christianity all about us. But the God who is on the throne of the universe and that you and I will one day stand before and give an account of our lives to, is not to be taken lightly!

BEFORE THE THRONE

Before the throne there are seven lamps of fire burning which are the seven spirits of God (4:5), and a sea of glass like crystal (4:6).

Seven lamps of fire

The seven lamps of fire symbolize the presence of the Holy Spirit in all his power. There is only one God, but this one God is three persons — God the Father, God the Son and God the Holy Spirit. Nowhere in the book of Revelation does John use the name Holy Spirit; but he uses the number seven to symbolize the Holy Spirit (1:4; 3:1; 4:5; 5:6), so when he talks of the seven spirits of God he is referring to the Holy Spirit. The number seven signifies the fulness and completeness of the Holy Spirit in his person and work.

Even though the Holy Spirit does not have a body, he is a real person. He teaches (John 14:26); testifies (John 15:26); convicts (John 16:8); guides (John 16:13); can be grieved (Ephesians 4:30); can be lied to (Acts 5:3). These are the actions of a real person, not a mere power or influence.

The work of the Holy Spirit is essential in a person becoming a Christian. You cannot be a Christian unless the Holy Spirit does a work in your heart. Only the Holy Spirit can produce a spiritual change in a person. The Bible says that we are all 'dead in trespasses and sins' (Ephesians 2:1, NKJV). Only the Holy Spirit can give us life. This is called regeneration. According to Packer, regeneration is 'God renovating the heart, the core of a person's being, by implanting a new principle of desire, purpose and action' (*Concise Theology*, p.157). It is a work which only God the Holy Spirit can do. Without the Holy Spirit we would have no interest in God. We would never put our faith in Jesus Christ or believe the gospel unless the Holy Spirit enabled us.

The first thing the Holy Spirit does that we are aware of is to convict us of our sin and show us our need to be saved. He then points us to Jesus Christ and gives us the faith to believe in him. After we become Christians the Holy Spirit lives within us and makes Jesus Christ more and more real to us and will give us a greater assurance of our faith. He produces within us the fruit of the Spirit which is 'love, joy, peace, patience, kindness, goodness, faithfulness, gentleness and self-control' (Galatians 5:22, NIV). As we read our Bibles, pray and seek to live lives which please God, this fruit will be cultivated and grow (John 15:1-7).

Pray that the Holy Spirit, symbolized by the seven lamps of fire before this throne, will give you the faith to believe in the one who sits on this throne, and the strength to live for him, and that you will have a desire to get to know him and love him more and more.

Sea of glass

The sea of glass conveys God's transcendence; he is above all created things and spiritually there is a vast distance between us and God. It is impossible for a human being on his or her own or by his or her own efforts to get anywhere near this awesome God. People think they can approach God and please him by their good works or their own efforts; but it is impossible. This is what all the religions are about — trying to reach God. Some people think that to please God they must confess their sins to another human being, bathe in a river, not eat during daylight for a month or go on a journey to a special place; but none of these endeavours, or any others, can enable me or you to approach the one who sits upon this throne. The distance between sinful, finite human beings and this holy, majestic, awesome God is too great.

AROUND THE THRONE

A rainbow

If all that John saw was a throne where a judge sat who was dazzlingly holy, dreadful in power and majesty, then this throne would be the last place you or I would dare to approach.

However, around the throne John saw a rainbow like an emerald (4:3). This rainbow illustrates the grace of God. We could never approach God on our own; but the good news is that by grace God has approached us!

Grace is the unmerited, undeserved favour of God to sinners. It is God being kind to people who deserve only judgement and condemnation. God's character is such that he cannot condone or overlook sin. His holiness demands that sin must be punished and the sinner dealt with. However, God is also love. He hates sin but loves the guilty sinner who deserves his judgement, so God's grace provides salvation for sinners. 'For God so loved the world that he gave his only begotten Son that whosoever believes in him should not perish but have everlasting life' (John 3:16, NKJV). This is all because of grace! Once a person understands grace, it is the most thrilling thing there is! I am a rotten, hell-deserving sinner, but God is gracious!

Because of grace you and I can know the holy, majestic, all-powerful one who sits upon the throne. We can approach this throne with confidence and may receive mercy and find grace to help in time of need (Hebrews 4:16).

Twenty-four elders and four living creatures

When we consider this throne and the one seated upon it, it is no wonder that all the creatures around this throne were worshipping. All we can do at the thought of one so holy, majestic, awesome, powerful and gracious is to bow in humble adoration.

Around the throne there were twenty-four elders sitting on twenty-four thrones in white garments, with golden crowns on their heads (4:4) and four living creatures (4:6).

The four creatures cry out: 'Holy, holy, holy is the Lord God Almighty, who was and is and is to come' (4:8, NIV). The twenty-four elders cast their crowns before him and fall down before him and ascribe him glory and honour and power because he created all things (4:11).

The reason the twenty-four elders and four creatures are around the throne is to enhance and underline the significance and importance of the throne.

In the Old Testament God's people were divided into twelve tribes, and in the New Testament the Lord Jesus Christ chose twelve apostles to follow him for three years and then to take the gospel into all the world. Thus twenty-four (the twelve apostles plus the twelve tribes of Israel) would represent the entire people of God, the church, from the Old and New Testament. The old and new dispensations are divided into the time before Jesus Christ came to this earth (Old Testament) and the time from his birth until he comes again (New Testament, plus subsequent church history). The elders wear white garments because they have been made clean and they have crowns on their heads because they are victorious.

The four living creatures are the most important of created beings. Not only are they around the throne, but in the centre (4:6), which emphasizes their closeness to God. In strength these creatures are like a lion, in service like an ox, in intelligence like a man and in swiftness like an eagle. There are four of them to show that all corners of the earth are covered; and they are full of eyes (4:6, 8) because they are always vigilant. They each have six wings (4:8) so they are always ready to obey and serve God. This throne is over the whole earth. Nobody and nowhere is outside the jurisdiction of this throne. This throne is above every other throne.

We also know from Revelation 5:13 that every creature in heaven and on earth and under the earth and on the sea, in fact everyone, is around this throne.

This vision of the throne would have really encouraged the first readers of this book. It showed them things as they really are. Caesar wasn't the real ruler of this world; the universe was governed by the throne in heaven and the one who sat on the throne wasn't evil but holy and gracious. Far from being weak and irrelevant, the God who they trusted was all-powerful and majestic.

If you're a Christian this throne in heaven should encourage you too. Maybe you are really struggling at the moment and facing overwhelming temptation. Perhaps you're thinking of giving up. Remember this throne in heaven! The one who sits on it is all-powerful and majestic and you can call on him at any time. The people who give you a hard time, and that particularly difficult situation you are going through, are all in his hand.

But if you are not a Christian, behold this throne! One day you will stand before it and the one who sits on it will judge you. He is the God 'to whom we must give account' (Hebrews 4:13, NKJV). Come to him now before it is too late, knowing that he is gracious and will receive anyone who comes to him in repentance and faith.

5

'WEEP NO MORE'

Revelation 5

In Revelation 4, John saw a door open in heaven, where he beheld a throne and the one sitting on the throne. Revelation 5 contains the second part of the vision of the throne.

We discover in Revelation 5:1 that the one sitting on the throne has a book in his right hand. This book is full of writing on both sides and is sealed up with seven seals. An angel proclaims with a loud voice: 'Who is worthy to open the book and to break its seals?' (5:2, NASB). However, no one in the entire universe is able to open the book or look into it. When John sees this he begins to weep greatly.

So what is contained in this book, and why does John weep so much when no one is able to open it?

THE BOOK

The book contains God's eternal plan. It concerns every creature and event throughout the whole of history. It is written on both sides because nothing is missing. It is complete. There are no holes in God's plan. Everyone and everything is included. The whole of human destiny and God's entire plan for the history of this world are in this book. Your life and my life are in this book.

SEALED

However, this book is sealed. Unless there is someone who can break and open these seven seals, God's purposes cannot be realized; his plan cannot be carried out. To open this book doesn't just require the ability to reveal God's plan, but the ability to carry out God's plan. An angel with a loud voice challenges the whole of creation to see if anyone can accomplish God's plan; but no one can.

WEEPS AND WEEPS AND WEEPS

When John sees that there is no one able to open this book, he weeps and weeps and weeps. He weeps so bitterly because if this book is not opened then God's plan cannot be executed and the universe will not be governed in the interest of the people of God, the church. There will be no ultimate triumph for believers; no help and protection in this life and no heaven in the next. There will be no forgiveness of sins. There will be no point to any of it if no one is found who can open this book.

John's tears encapsulate the whole frustration of the human race. They resonate with the big questions and issues that we have deep inside us: What's the point of it all? What happens when I die? Why is there so much evil? How can I get rid of my guilt?

William Shakespeare epitomizes this frustration in his play *Macbeth* when he says life is 'a poor player that struts and frets his hour upon the stage and then is heard no more: it is a tale told by an idiot, full of sound and fury, signifying nothing'. The seeming pointlessness and hopelessness of it all!

WEEP NO MORE

While John is sobbing his heart out at the hopelessness of the plight of mankind, one of the elders tells him to stop weeping. He says to him, 'Behold, the Lion that is from the tribe of Judah, the Root of David, has overcome so as to open the book and its seven seals' (5:5, NASB). Someone has been found who can open the book and accomplish the plan of God! This one is none other than the Lord Jesus Christ. According to Lloyd-Jones: 'Our Lord is the Lord of history. He controls it; he is its Master. And I know nothing more consoling!' (*The Church and the Last Things*, p.179).

In the Old Testament the people of God were divided into twelve tribes. Each tribe was named after one of the twelve sons of Jacob (also known as Israel). One of these tribes was called Judah. From this tribe came Israel's greatest king, David. In the genealogy of Jesus Christ (Matthew 1) we see that Jesus descends from the line of David and from the tribe of Judah. Here Jesus Christ is described as the 'lion from the tribe of Judah', which is a reference to Genesis 49:9. The title depicts Christ as the culmination of courage, might and ferocity. Christ is pictured as a conquering lion.

But what is this lion of the tribe of Judah coming to overcome? In a word, sin. This is the cause of all the problems in the world today, as it has been from the beginning and will be right up to the end. God created man and woman perfect. They were made in the image of God. This means that we have the capacity to know and enjoy God. This fellowship was shattered by what is known as the Fall.

The events are related in Genesis 3. God placed the first man and woman, Adam and Eve, in a garden called Eden. It was paradise.

They could eat of any fruit in the garden except from the tree of the knowledge of good and evil. If they ate from this tree they would surely die (Genesis 2:17). It was a clear command and warning from God. However, the devil came to Eve in the form of a serpent and deceived her into eating the forbidden fruit. She in turn gave some to Adam. Adam and Eve thus disobeyed God, and sin and death entered the world. The apostle Paul says in Romans 5:12 (NIV), 'Sin entered the world through one man, and death through sin, and in this way death came to all men, because all sinned.' The Fall did not only affect Adam and Eve, but the entire human race. Adam was our representative, so sin is part of the nature of all of us. The consequences of sin and the Fall are enormous. It has separated us from God; it makes us dirty; it affects our minds and our actions and pollutes every part of our nature. Evil entered the world. We lost eternal life and instead face eternal damnation. According to Packer: 'It may fairly be claimed that the fall narrative gives the only convincing explanation of the perversity of human nature that the world has ever seen' (*Concise Theology*, p.81).

Peter Jeffery concurs with this view: 'The story of Adam and Eve is generally regarded as a myth today. That is a tragic mistake, for the events recorded in that chapter have a greater bearing on your life today than anything that is currently happening. It is here that we have the origin of sin in man's nature' (*Christian Handbook*, p.142).

Furthermore, not only did humankind fall but the whole of creation is now under a curse. This explains the natural disasters that occur and cause such devastation.

A LAMB (5:6)

However, when John looks again, he doesn't see a lion, but a lamb that had been slain, covered in blood. God's plan for humanity would be accomplished through the sacrifice of a lamb. The problem of sin and all the results of the Fall would be dealt with by a lamb.

The symbol of the lamb comes from the lamb slain for the Passover. God's people in the Old Testament were slaves in Egypt. God sent Moses to tell Pharaoh to let his people go but Pharaoh refused. God sent ten plagues to change his mind; but each time Pharaoh refused; until the last plague, the death of the eldest son. God sent an angel of death to Egypt to kill the eldest son in every Egyptian household. God's people were told to kill a lamb and put its blood on the sides and top of the door frame of their houses. When the angel saw the blood he would know to 'pass over'. The blood of the lamb saved the people. In the Old Testament, lambs were sacrificed to take away the sins of the people. These all were types and shadows of the Lamb of God who would one day come to take away the sin of the world (John 1:29; Isaiah 53:7-8). He did this by dying on the cross two thousand years ago at a place called Golgotha outside the city wall of Jerusalem.

The lamb John sees has seven horns and seven eyes. The seven horns symbolize the fulness of Christ's power and the seven eyes the fact that there is no area over which he does not sovereignly have control. Abraham Kuyper of Holland (1837-1920) said, 'There is not a square inch in the whole domain of our human existence over which Jesus Christ, who is sovereign over all, does not cry "mine".'

The key to the whole of history is the cross of Jesus Christ. The lion/lamb is the pivotal point in everything. This is what gives history its meaning. International events, national events and personal circumstances all find their meaning in the cross of Jesus Christ. All of life's problems — its suffering and its sin — are dealt with on the cross. It is so important in the history of the world that Jesus Christ refers to it as 'my hour' or 'the hour'.

On the cross Jesus Christ poured out his blood to purchase people for God from every tribe and language and people and nation (5:9).

Because of all that the Lord Jesus Christ had accomplished, the four creatures and the twenty-four elders and many angels numbering thousands upon thousands and ten thousands upon ten thousands and every creature in heaven and on the earth and under the earth and on the sea worshipped him (5:11-14). In other words, the whole of creation worships the Lamb.

THE PRAYERS OF THE SAINTS

But the church is not yet complete. There are still more people to be saved; so in verse 8 the four living creatures and the twenty-four elders were holding golden bowls of incense which are the prayers of the saints. ('Saint' is a title given to every person who trusts in Jesus Christ.)

The prayers of the saints are the most important events in history. Never mind cabinet meetings and summits between international leaders, the most important meetings on earth are prayer meetings where ordinary people pour out their hearts to almighty God and make intercession for others. This is where the power of God is to be found.

Maybe you find prayer difficult and the prayer meeting hard work and boring. But we should always pray and not give up, because prayer changes things. The period between the first and second coming of Jesus Christ is sometimes referred to as the gospel age. The most important and essential thing we can do during this gospel age is pray.

We should pray for conversions, for our churches, that we would become more holy, to have assurance that we are really Christians and loved by God. We should take God's promises in the Bible and pray them back to him.

We can also pray for personal things. Through prayer we can cast all our care upon him because he cares for us (1 Peter 5:7) — relationships, exams, careers, family. We can rest in the knowledge that even when our prayers are not answered as we would like them to be it is because God has a better plan for us. If we seek him with all our hearts we will find him and when we call out to him and pray to him he will listen (Jeremiah 29:11-13).

We should also pray for revival. God is always with his people; but during a period of revival God comes down among his people in a very special, tangible way. His presence can be felt. The church is revived, people are saved and the community as a whole is affected and transformed. Duncan Campbell described a revival as a 'community saturated with God' (quoted in Edwards, *Revival — a people saturated with God*, p.26). Surely we should be pleading with God for times like this!

Let me encourage you to attend the prayer meeting in your church and to pray! Plead with God to revive his church once again. We seem to have lost faith in the power of prayer and don't spend enough time really seeking God. I'm sure that at ten past nine on a Wednesday night, or whenever your weekly prayer meeting is, heaven must think, 'Is that it? Is that all you're going to ask for tonight?' Let's really seek him! In 2 Chronicles 7:14 (NASB) God promises that if 'my people who are called by my name humble themselves and pray and seek my face and turn from their wicked ways, then I will hear from heaven, will forgive their sin and will heal their land'.

Prayer meetings are the most important meetings on earth because the all-powerful God listens to the prayers of his people.

6

SEVEN SEALS

Revelation 6

A t the start of this chapter it is probably worth noting that
whereas we categorize people in many different ways — rich
and poor, educated and uneducated, sporty and un-sporty, black
and white, male and female, religious and non-religious, moral and
immoral, upper class, middle class and working class, and so on —
in God's eyes there are two groups of people. These two groups of
people are described in different ways — those who trust him and
those who don't; those who are for him and those who are against
him; the righteous and the wicked; his followers and his enemies;
believers and unbelievers; saints and sinners.

From the perspective of heaven and throughout this revelation
there are simply these two groups of people. The important question
for you is which group do you belong to? As we go through this
book you will see more and more the importance of this question
to your eternal destiny.

THE OPENING OF THE SEALS

In chapter 6 the Lamb opens the seals of the book that is in the right hand of God, who is seated on the throne (chapter 5). It is important to keep in our minds that this vision is still in the throne-room of heaven. The twenty-four elders and four living creatures are still part of this vision.

The opening of the seals is an unveiling of the history of the world and the church. It is the events we read about on the pages of our newspapers every day, only here we see them in their true light. Every major event that happens in our country is covered by all the daily newspapers; but they are not all reported in the same way. Each paper puts its own slant on the story. Here we have the history of the world as it really is, as viewed and directed from the throne of the universe.

This history covers the period between Christ's ascension and his second coming. In summary, during this period the gospel advances to the ends of the earth, wars devastate its population, famines cause endless suffering, and death is the constant companion to those who dwell on the earth; and all the while those who live godly lives suffer persecution.

The first four seals form a unit that features four coloured horses. The fifth seal portrays souls under the altar and represents people who died for their faith in the Lord Jesus Christ. The sixth seal depicts the judgement and the terror of those who reject Jesus Christ. The seventh seal does not come until the beginning of chapter 8: there is an interlude in chapter 7 between the sixth and seventh seals.

THE FIRST FOUR SEALS

When the first four seals are opened John sees four horses and their riders.

The *first horse* was white. Its rider held a bow. He was given a crown and he rode out as a conqueror bent on conquest (7:2). There is some debate as to who the rider on the white horse is; but it would appear that the white horse and its rider represent the Lord Jesus Christ and the advancement of his gospel. In Revelation 19:11 Christ is riding on a white horse; the symbolism of the colour white in Revelation refers to what is pure and holy; in Revelation 14:14 Christ is wearing a crown of gold; almost everywhere in the book of Revelation the words '*to conquer*' refer to Christ or his followers; and the emphasis throughout the book is on Christ the conqueror. It seems, then, that the first horse and its rider represent Christ and the advancement of his gospel. We can see this throughout the history of the church from the time of the New Testament up to the present time and until Christ returns to this world.

This horse and its rider first advanced in Jerusalem, then Judea and Samaria, and then to the uttermost parts of the world. The horse and its rider have advanced throughout history: first through the preaching and ministry of the disciples and the early church and then through the martyrs, the church fathers, John Wycliffe, Martin Luther, John Calvin, the Puritans, the Wesleys, George Whitefield, Charles Spurgeon, William Carey, David Livingstone, and Hudson Taylor, to name but a few. By today, every nation has heard the gospel.

Nothing can prevent the white horse and its rider advancing. This is clearly seen in China. Under Mao Tse-Tung the church was persecuted and Christianity almost disappeared. But the country has experienced possibly the biggest revival in history and Tony Lambert has written about 'China's Christian millions'. Years of persecution and harsh oppression failed to destroy Christianity. It has grown at an enormous rate in the last few decades.

The *second horse* was a fiery red one. Its rider was given power to take peace from the earth and to make men slay each other. He was given a large sword (7:4). This horse and its rider represent wars. Throughout the history of this world there will always be wars. In Matthew 24:6-7 (NIV) the Lord Jesus says, 'You will hear of wars and rumours of wars, but see to it that you are not alarmed. Such things must happen, but the end is still to come. Nation will rise against nation and kingdom against kingdom.'

We hear and see this every day on our televisions and in our newspapers. It has been estimated that in the last four thousand years there have been less than three hundred years without a major war. Thirty million people were killed in World War I, while the figures for World War II are so vast that they have never been accurately computed. At one point, opponents of Mao Tse-Tung's Communist Revolution in China were being executed at the rate of 22,000 a month. Pol Pot slaughtered over 1.5 million Cambodians in less than two years. In the six weeks from 7 April 1994 over half a million Rwandans were massacred in the savage civil war between Hutus and Tutsis.

However, even though the traditional way of interpreting the red horse is to understand it as symbolizing war between nations, it could also be possible that the red horse refers to the persecution of the church rather than to war between nations. The red horse follows the white horse, which would fit in with what we read of in church history and what we see today. Wherever the gospel is preached and believed, persecution follows hard after it.

The *third horse* was black. Its rider was holding a pair of scales in his hand. A voice came out from one of the four living creatures saying, 'A quart of wheat for a day's wages and three quarts of barley for a day's wages, and do not damage the oil and the wine' (7:6, NIV). This describes famine. The prices quoted for the wheat are famine prices which were twelve times the ordinary rate. A man's wage would only buy enough wheat to support himself, and if he wanted to provide for his family he would have to buy barley instead. Out of his day's wage, which would have been a denarius, he could afford a quart of wheat but could get three quarts of barley. Again, famine has been present throughout the history of the world and is still present today. Jesus told us so in Matthew 24:7 (NIV) when he said, 'There will be famines and earthquakes in various places.'

However, the oil and the wine are not damaged. Even though the poor struggle to survive, the rich still enjoy the comforts of life.

Even though the third horse is traditionally seen as famine, some renowned Bible commentators, such as Hendriksen, believe that as with the second horse it refers specifically to the church. He believes the two horses should be taken together; and whereas the red horse symbolizes the outward physical persecution which some Christians suffer, the black horse symbolizes the hardships and difficulties a Christian will face. The first readers of this letter would have known only too well these hardships. Belonging to the trade guilds required them to sacrifice their Christian principles; and if they didn't, they would no doubt experience material loss. Today, many Christians suffer because they refuse to work on a Sunday or compromise their beliefs to climb the 'greasy pole'. Maybe you are finding it difficult being a Christian in school, university or at work because of activities that other people are getting involved in but you can't because you are a Christian. You feel a bit lonely and weird and left out. This type of subtle, yet very real, persecution could very well be pictured here by the black horse.

The *fourth horse* is pale, a kind of greenish yellowish horse. Its rider was named Death, and Hades was following close behind him. They were given power over a fourth of the earth to kill by sword, famine and plague, and by the wild beasts of the earth. This horse symbolizes death and all the woes common to man, Christian and non-Christian.

Death is always closely followed by Hades. However, they do not have free rein. They were given power by God only over a fourth of the earth. All wars, plagues, disasters, pestilences, even death are in God's hand. Whereas they affect ungodly people for their eternal damnation, when they affect believers they are working for their eternal good.

In other words, suffering and death will come to all people — those who trust in Jesus Christ and those who don't. For those who do not trust in him, they bring eternal damnation and suffering. For those who do trust in him, they are the entrance to paradise and being with Jesus Christ for ever.

To illustrate this point let's take the example of the wild beasts mentioned in verse 8. In the first century, when this book was written, wild beasts would kill and devour whatever they could seize. These same wild beasts were used by the Romans to kill Christians in the amphitheatres. Houghton gives examples of these Christian martyrs (*Sketches from Church History*, pp. 17-18). He tells of Ignatius of Antioch, who was thrown to the wild beasts because of his faith in Jesus. Face to face with death, Ignatius said, 'I am God's grain, to be ground between the teeth of wild beasts, so that I may become a holy loaf for the Lord.' Soon after the lions were loosed upon him, nothing was left but a few gnawed bones. When his friends came to collect his bones for burial, they knew that Ignatius was 'with Christ, which is far better' (Philippians 1:23, NKJV).

Another example is Polycarp of Smyrna who refused to say that Caesar was lord and was sentenced to death by the Roman consul. He was threatened with wild beasts and with fire but remained faithful to the Lord Jesus. He is reported to have said, 'Eighty and six years have I served Christ and he has done me no wrong; how can I blaspheme my king who has saved me? You threaten the fire that burns for an hour and then is quenched; but you know not of the fire of eternal punishment. Bring what you will.'

When the torch was applied to the wood, and smoke and flames encircled him, he thanked God for being deemed worthy to receive the crown of martyrdom. It is recorded that the multitude who were watching marvelled at the great difference between Christians and non-Christians.

Disasters and difficulties are the lot of every human being; but for Christians even these things work for their eternal good.

THE FIFTH SEAL

When the fifth seal was opened, John saw under the altar the souls of those who had been martyred for their faith in Jesus Christ. They were crying out to God to see how long it would be before he judged the inhabitants of the earth and avenged their blood. They were each given a white robe and were told to wait a little longer until the number of the martyrs was complete (6:9-11).

The martyrs are clothed in white robes, which symbolize their holiness and righteousness. These martyrs were sinners just like you and me; but because of their faith in Jesus Christ they are now spotlessly pure. These martyrs had suffered greatly for their faith, to the point of death; but now they are perfectly safe and happy under the altar which is at the bottom of God's throne. In his *Book of Martyrs*, Foxe describes the dramatic stories of some of these Christian martyrs. Mark, who wrote one of the Gospels, was dragged to pieces by the people of Alexandria, ending his life at their merciless hands. Luke, who wrote another of the Gospels, was hanged on an olive tree by the idolatrous priests of Greece. According to tradition, Peter, one of the Lord Jesus' twelve disciples, was crucified upside down. Others throughout history have been fed to the lions, burnt at the stake, beheaded, killed by the sword, or (more recently) shot.

However, even though the enemies of the gospel killed their bodies, they live on in heaven. Their enemies had no power to destroy their souls. Jesus tells us not to fear those who can destroy our bodies; rather fear him who has the power to destroy both our bodies and souls in hell.

It is also a great comfort to know that God knows the exact number of the martyrs. Those who die for Jesus Christ, his shock troops against evil, are known to him and each one is precious. We live at a time when people are just numbers and statistics. But 'precious in the eyes of the LORD is the death of his godly ones' (Psalm 116:15, NASB).

They are eager for God to avenge their blood. They want the enemies of the gospel to be judged and have their comeuppance. They are told to exercise patience and accept that God sovereignly controls world history. Not until all God's people are safely under the throne of God will he finally judge the wicked.

It is important to realize that the martyrs do not want retribution for their own sakes but for God's sake. According to Hendriksen:

> These saints have been slaughtered because they placed their trust and confidence in God. In slaughtering them, the world has scorned Him! Insignificant individuals, mere earth dwellers, have defied the holy, true and sovereign Lord of the universe. They have challenged His attributes. Unless full retribution be rendered, God's righteousness and sovereignty will not shine forth in its full and perfect lustre ... the saint in glory does not desire personal vengeance ... but he yearns for the coming of that great day when the majesty and holiness,

the sovereignty and righteousness of God in Christ shall be publicly revealed

(*More Than Conquerors*, p.106).

The saints want justice!

THE SIXTH SEAL — JUDGEMENT DAY

As the sixth seal is opened, John sees what will happen at the end of time. Verses 12-17 symbolically describe the physical catastrophes which will take place at the end of the world when unbelievers face the wrath of God and the Lamb. At this time there will be an earthquake, the sun will become black, the moon become like blood and stars will fall from the sky. It will be terrifying for everyone who is not safe under the throne of God. The kings of the earth, princes, great men, commanders, the rich, the strong, slaves and the free, in fact every kind of person will be so afraid that they will try to hide in caves and want the mountains to fall on them. The question will go out: 'Who can stand?' (7:17).

These things are real and will definitely come to pass. The judgement of God and hell awaits everyone who does not trust in the only Saviour of mankind, Jesus Christ. In the twenty-first century even Bible-believing Christians have tried to sanitize hell and cover it up as some kind of embarrassing family secret; but hell is as real and terrifying today as it has always been. As you sit reading this book, wherever you may be, there are people who once walked this earth and lived and breathed like you, but now find themselves in torment in hell. Conversely, Polycarp and Ignatius and the other martyrs are safely beneath the throne of God, waiting for the sixth seal to be opened. Make sure you are right with the one who sits on the throne and are trusting in the Lamb that was slain!

7

'A GREAT MULTITUDE
WHICH NO ONE COULD NUMBER'

Revelation 7

In Revelation 6 the Lamb opens the book that was in the right hand of the one who sat upon the throne. The book was sealed with seven seals, and by the end of the sixth chapter six of the seven seals had been opened. The seventh seal isn't opened until chapter 8. Therefore chapter 7 functions as an important interlude. At the end of chapter 6, in the face of such terrifying judgements, the question went up: 'Who can stand?' In chapter 7 we are given a vision which answers that question. The first 8 verses are viewed from the aspect of earth and verse 9 onwards from the aspect of heaven.

At the beginning of chapter 7, everything seems ready for the execution of the judgements described at the end of chapter 6. John sees four angels who are controlling the winds of judgement that are about to sweep through the whole earth (7:1). It seems they are just waiting for the go-ahead to unleash these catastrophic judgements on the world. But dramatically, John sees another angel ascending from the east (7:2). He has the seal of the living God and he calls out with a loud voice to the four angels who had been given power to harm the land and the sea: 'Do not harm the land or sea or the trees until we put a seal on the foreheads of the servants of our God' (7:3, NIV). Not everyone will suffer these terrifying judgements. God's people must be sealed.

A seal has a threefold purpose. It protects against tampering, it marks ownership, and it certifies genuine character. All Christians are sealed in these three ways. They enjoy the protection of God the Father throughout their lives; God the Son owns them because he bought them with his own precious blood; God the Holy Spirit has sealed every Christian (Ephesians 1:13) because he certifies that we are the sons of God (Romans 8:15).

The number of the sealed is 144,000. This number is symbolic. It equals the twelve tribes of Israel times the twelve apostles times a thousand. The twelve apostles times the twelve tribes of Israel represent the entire people of God, the church, from the Old and New Testament. The thousand signifies a large multitude, or even a cube (10x10x10), which symbolizes completeness. The number represents the complete number of God's people, more than any man can number (7:9) from the old and new dispensations.

The judgements to come mentioned at the end of chapter 6 will not harm the people sealed by God.

The number 144,000 is a symbolic description of the sealed, but in Revelation 7:9-10 an actual description is given of them. They are a great multitude which no one could number from all nations, tribes, peoples and tongues. They stand before the throne and before the Lamb clothed in white robes, with palm branches in their hands, and they cry out with a loud voice saying, 'Salvation belongs to our God who sits on the throne and to the Lamb' (7:10, NIV).

This great multitude consists of everyone who has trusted, does trust, or ever will trust in the Lord Jesus Christ to save them. It is the same multitude which was once in a pitiable state, the ones who have come out of the tribulation (7:14). This multitude was once a minority, marginalized, misunderstood and mistreated by the world. At their worst they could be evangelically ineffective, spiritually dying, morally lax and doctrinally compromised. They struggled with the pressure of the outside world and faced economic oppression, social exclusion and even the threat of physical violence because they were Christians. The multitude includes the Christians in the seven churches in chapters 2 and 3 of Revelation; all Christians throughout church history; Christians today, including me and you.

We are all pictured here, not struggling with trials, temptations and sin, but in the immediate presence of God! This awesome God, who sits on the throne of the whole universe, treats all who trust his Son as his own dear children. Never again will we hunger; never again will we thirst; the sun will not beat upon us or any scorching heat. We will be led by the Lamb to springs of living water and God will wipe away every tear from our eyes (7:16-17).

Can you imagine how the first readers of this book would have felt when they read these great promises? Even though they were suffering, eternal paradise with God awaited them! They would have agreed with the apostle Paul when he said, 'I consider that our present sufferings are not worth comparing with the glory that will be revealed in us' (Romans 8:18, NIV).

It resonates with the words of the old Negro spirituals: despite being slaves, they had a 'home in glory land that outshines the sun'. Or think of the group of coalminers from Kingswood near Bristol in the eighteenth century. These men lived in some of the most wretched living conditions in England at that time. They lived in hovels, dens and holes in the earth (Dallimore, *George Whitefield*, vol. 1, p.256). They spent their days burrowing in the hills and were covered in coal dust and black as soot. When Wesley and Whitefield were preaching to them, the first signs that they were being affected by the gospel were the white streaks on their faces where the tears ran down their cheeks. John Wesley wrote a hymn for these filthy men to sing as they came out of their holes in the ground. The last verse says:

> With him we walk in white,
> We in his image shine,
> Our robes are robes of glorious light,
> Our righteousness divine;
> On all the kings of earth
> With pity we look down,
> And claim, in virtue of our birth,
> A never ending crown.

These eighteenth-century miners are no longer in filthy holes in the earth but as you are reading this book they are in the very presence of God and the Lamb!

The multitude described in this chapter is made up of all kinds of people: black and white; middle class and working class; rich and poor; educated and uneducated; Africans, Americans, Europeans, Asians; men and women, boys and girls; teenagers, middle-aged people, pensioners; people who lived at the very beginning of time right up to twenty-first-century people. What a mixed bag!

But now they are all in white garments. They have all been saved by the Lamb. None of them deserves to be among this great gathering, which is why their song is: 'Salvation belongs to our God and to the Lamb.' This great multitude is no better in and of themselves than the ones who face the terrible judgement of God. The only

difference is that God has set his love upon this multitude. He
has graciously saved them. We have done nothing to contribute
towards our salvation. We were dead in trespasses and sin and
could do nothing to save ourselves. We would never have chosen
God.

The biblical doctrine of election is that before creation God selected
out of the human race people he would save. God owes sinners
no mercy of any kind, only condemnation; it is the reason why
the saints around the throne in heaven are so full of praise. Why
should he choose to save any of us?

The doctrine of election has caused some controversy, but it is not
unfair. God does not punish anyone unjustly. We are all sinners by
nature and deserve God's wrath. But God in his mercy saves some
and in his justice condemns others. The one who is condemned
must acknowledge that he is receiving only what his sin deserves. It
is important to remember that no one has been sent to hell because
he was not elect. People are in hell because they would not come
to Jesus Christ. No sinner has ever come to Jesus Christ and been
turned away. No one will be able to say to Jesus Christ on judgement
day, 'I called to you but you would not listen.' Even though election
is on every page of the Bible, it is equally true that 'Whoever calls
on the name of the Lord shall be saved' (Acts 2:21, NKJV) and
that God takes 'no pleasure in the death of the wicked, but rather
that the wicked turn from his way and live' (Ezekiel 33:11, NASB).
Whoever wants to can come to Jesus Christ!

If you are not part of this great multitude, come now! Come as you
are, confessing your sin. Your past will be forgiven and forgotten;
you'll have a guide, a friend and protector through life, and a
glorious hope for the future!

SECTION 3

Seven trumpets

(Revelation 8 - 11)

8

SILENCE IN HEAVEN

Revelation 8:1-5

In Revelation 8:1 the seventh seal is opened. This seal is the judgement of unbelievers. Seven angels are given seven trumpets (8:2), which are going to herald remarkable disasters. They are warning judgements and pictures of God's judgement and patience.

But before these trumpets are blown we read these remarkable words, 'there was silence in heaven for about half an hour' (8:1, NIV).

Why was heaven silent for about half an hour?

One reason could be that the whole of heaven was awestruck at the prospect of the judgement of God. Many people today think that if there is a God and they one day will stand before him, they'll say this to him and that to him. People talk about God as though he is just a topic for intellectual discussion and academic debate. Others use his name as a swear-word and treat him as a joke. Others couldn't care less. But when a creature is before this awesome God they will be awestruck. Imagine standing next to God when he created the world, or when he crushed his Son on Golgotha, or when, as here, he judges the world. You and I will be silent!

But this silence could also be because prayers are being offered up to heaven. This may be a view of prayer from the vantage point of heaven. We may feel our prayers are pointless and just a means of us getting things off our chests. We may have sat through prayer meetings which we have felt have been dry and boring, and we don't see any answers to our prayers. But in heaven there has been silence because some of God's people on earth are crying out to him.

You may think to yourself: what is the point of me praying? But your prayer ascends to the very throne of God (8:3-5). He stills heaven, as it were, to listen to the prayers of his people. Prayer lies at the very centre of his relationship with his people.

John sees that an angel came and stood at the altar and was given much incense to offer (v. 3). It seems that this incense which the angel is given represents our Saviour's intercession in heaven on behalf of his people.

A preacher once came to preach at the Heath Evangelical Church in Cardiff and gave a very memorable illustration of this. He said that his niece came in from the garden where she had picked flowers for her mother. What the little girl actually had in her hand was a clump of earth with some flowers mixed up with weeds. Her sentiment was lovely in that she wanted to bring something nice for her mother. The preacher said he spent time with the little girl picking out the weeds and getting rid of the earth to make the flowers a presentable posy for her mother. That is a picture of what Jesus Christ does with our prayers. We come to God in prayer, our theology not always correct; stumbling and stammering; repeating ourselves and not really saying what we want to. But in heaven there's a man, the God-man Jesus Christ, who intercedes on our behalf and makes our prayers acceptable to God.

The prayers of the saints, together with the incense, were set ablaze with the fire of God and hurled onto the earth.

Prayer moves the whole course of world history! This was dramatically seen in Germany in 1989 when the Berlin wall was brought down. A group of young people had been praying about the situation in East Germany for some time in the Lutheran Church where Johann Sebastian Bach was once the organist. These young people were joined by their parents and grandparents and eventually there were over ten thousand people from different Christian denominations (groups) praying. They could not fit into the church, so they held their meetings in the square outside the church. The government heard of the meetings and sent the army in to kill, if necessary: anything to break up the meeting and disperse the crowd. When the army arrived they saw members of their own families there — mothers, wives, children — and refused to follow orders. The dictators had lost control of the army. As I'm sure you know, oppressive rulers and dictators rely completely on their control of the police and the army. Once they've lost that, they've lost their power. The following morning, they began pulling the wall down!

Men, women, and young people ought always to pray!

9

SEVEN TRUMPETS

Revelation 8:6 - 11:19

SUMMARY

The first four trumpets belong together and are found in Revelation 8:6-13. They are largely concerned with nature.

Between the first four trumpets and the fifth and sixth trumpets an eagle flies in mid heaven uttering the word 'woe' because of the dreadfulness of the trumpets that are to follow.

The fifth and sixth trumpets are found in Revelation 9.

The seventh trumpet isn't sounded until Revelation 11:15, after an interlude from Revelation 10:1 - 11:14 which describes the persecution the church will face during these trumpet blasts and the fact that it will suffer for preaching the gospel. Even so, it will be safe and unharmed.

THE FIRST FOUR TRUMPETS (REVELATION 8:6-13)

The trumpets are simultaneous with the seals. They cover the same ground but from a different point of view. Revelation is not chronological; that is, Revelation 8:6-13 does not take place after Revelation 6. These events happen at the same time. It is the same picture but from a different angle and is meant to teach us something different. It puts a different slant on what is happening.

With the trumpets there is now an increasing intensity. God gave the seals a fourth part of the earth (6:8), whereas the trumpets are given a third of the earth (8:7-12).

The trumpets are God's judgements on the world. Human wickedness does not go unnoticed in heaven and the trumpets are to warn people of this.

Similar to the plagues in Egypt

These judgements are similar to the plagues that God sent to Egypt in the book of Exodus.

His purpose in sounding the trumpets is the same as in sending those plagues. A trumpet is sounded to herald or announce something and can be used in the same way as a horn, to warn us. God sounds these trumpets to alert the world to important matters; matters of life, death, judgement and eternity.

God's people were slaves in Egypt and God sent Moses to Pharaoh to tell him to let his people go. Pharaoh refused so God sent a series of judgements — water turning to blood, a plague of frogs, two plagues of insects, death of the cattle, a plague of boils, hail, locusts, darkness over the land and the death of the eldest son in every Egyptian family (Exodus 7:14 – 11:10). The judgements John sees resemble the Egyptian plagues but are even more dramatic. For example, the fourth plague in Egypt was hail and fire (Exodus 9:23-26), whereas when the first trumpet is sounded hail and fire mixed with blood were hurled down upon the earth.

The purpose of the trumpets is the same as that of the plagues in Egypt. God sent the plagues upon Egypt to move Pharaoh to repentance. God wants everyone to repent. According to Packer:

> *Repentance means changing one's mind so that one's views, values, goals and ways are changed and one's whole life is lived differently. The change is radical, both inwardly and outwardly; mind and judgment, will and affections, behaviour and lifestyle, motives and purposes, are all involved. Repenting means starting to live a new life*
>
> (*Concise Theology*, p.162).

These devastating plagues were God's way of pleading with Pharaoh to stop fighting against him. It was the only way to make him take note. However, even then, each time a plague was sent Pharaoh hardened his heart towards God until, chillingly, God hardened Pharaoh's heart! (*cf*. Exodus 8:32; 9:12). God pleads for so long, but will finally say that enough is enough!

The only part of Egypt most of the plagues didn't touch was Goshen, where God's people were. The plagues did not harm them. In the same way, these disasters cannot harm the saints.

Not to be taken literally

What these trumpet blasts describe is not to be taken literally. Lenski (*The Interpretation of St John's Revelation*) believes that the six trumpet blasts in chapters 8 and 9 should be taken as a whole. It is not really possible to say the exact meaning of every feature from the trumpet blasts; the important point is the effect the trumpets have. The judgements the trumpets describe get worse each time. Judgement is restrained as much as possible. The severity of the judgements increases only as people continually refuse to repent and take note of the warnings. God may send judgements upon nations or individuals to warn them that they are not, to quote W. E. Henley (1849–1903), 'the master of their own fate or the captain of their soul'. Man is not in control. When the *Titanic* set sail it was the largest moveable object ever made by man and said to be so well built that 'God himself couldn't sink the ship'. However, on her maiden voyage she struck an iceberg in the North Atlantic and sank with the loss of 1,500 lives.

We are answerable and accountable to God. We were made by him and live in his world; yet we treat it as we like and think we can do what we want. God sends preachers to command people to repent. He offers them a Saviour who can save to the uttermost all who will come to him; but people wilfully and arrogantly refuse. So God sends suffering or disaster on nations or individuals to warn them more dramatically to repent. He does this not because he is cruel but because he is merciful. If he were cruel, he would not warn us at all, but simply send us immediately to hell. But it is his will that none should perish (2 Peter 3:9). C. S. Lewis said that suffering and disasters are like God's megaphone to rouse a sinful, unrepenting world.

The first trumpet sounded, and hail and fire mixed with blood were hurled down upon the earth. A third of the earth and a third of the trees were burned up, as was all the grass (8:7).

The second trumpet sounded and something like a huge mountain on fire was thrown into the sea. A third of the sea turned into blood, a third of the living creatures in the sea died and a third of the ships were destroyed (8:8-9).

On the third trumpet sound a great star called Wormwood, blazing like a torch, fell from the sky on a third of the rivers and on the springs of water. A third of the waters turned bitter and many people died from the waters that had become bitter.

When the fourth angel sounded his trumpet, a third of the sun, a third of the moon, and a third of the stars turned dark; which meant that a third of the day and the night were without light.

The meaning is clear. God uses the earth, seas, rivers and solar system to execute judgement. He is in control of them all.

God controls everything, even natural disasters, and uses them to warn people that there is a God in heaven to whom we must all answer. Each trumpet blast is a warning for people to repent; that is, turn from their sin and turn to God. It is also a reminder that, as a result of the Fall, the whole of creation is cursed.

The pictures described in these first four trumpets are terrible; but if we think of all the devastation caused by disasters on the land and sea throughout the centuries, these visions have not been exaggerated.

Earthquakes, volcanoes, floods, hurricanes, tidal waves, fires and other natural disasters have killed or injured millions of people, often wiping out huge numbers within a few hours.

20,000 people perished in an earthquake in China's Kansu province in 1920. 12,000 were drowned and millions made homeless when Hurricane Mitch hit South America in 1998. More recently, Pakistan experienced floods which have left a trail of destruction along the Indus river basin, from the mountainous north to the Punjab, and the plains of Sindh province in the south. Some 2.6 million acres of cropland were under water and thousands of people were stranded. It is on a scale too difficult for most of us to grasp. Fourteen million people were affected and the death toll on 14 August 2010 stood at 1,600. In February 2010 an earthquake ravaged Haiti, killing 200,000 people. These are God's trumpets to warn and remind us that this world is under a curse as the result of the Fall and that there is a God in heaven with whom we have to do!

The fourth trumpet is also a reminder to all the people obsessed with looking to the stars for guidance that the whole solar system is controlled by God. He named every star, so he is the one we should look to for guidance. We do that by looking in his Word, the Bible, and coming to him in prayer.

After the fourth trumpet is sounded John sees an eagle flying in mid air. The eagle warns that the next three trumpets will be even more frightening (Revelation 8:13).

THE FIFTH AND SIXTH TRUMPETS (REVELATION 9)

Fifth trumpet (9:1-11)

When the fifth trumpet is sounded John sees a star that has fallen out of heaven to earth. This star is Satan. In Luke 10:18 the Lord Jesus Christ says, 'I saw Satan fall like lightning from heaven' (NKJV). Satan was an angel in heaven; but he rebelled against God and was cast out. Having lost his splendour and position in heaven, he roams the earth.

In this vision he is given the key to the shaft of the abyss. The abyss is hell before the final judgement. After the judgement hell is called the lake of fire (Revelation 20:14-15). When Satan opens the shaft of the abyss he fills the world with demons and with their wicked influences and actions. As soon as the shaft is unlocked smoke comes out of it like the smoke from a gigantic furnace.

According to Hendriksen: 'It is the smoke of deception and delusion, of sin and sorrow, of moral darkness and degradation that is constantly belching up out of hell' (*More Than Conquerors*, p.120).

Out of the smoke locusts descend on the earth (9:3). Locusts cause terrible devastation and destruction. However, these are no ordinary locusts. They don't destroy or harm vegetation; they harm all people who have not been sealed. In 9:7-11 we have a graphic description of these hellish locusts. The description should be taken as a whole. The image it portrays is frightful, horrible but true. It is the powers and influences of hell in the souls of the wicked. This wickedness is most clearly seen in the actions of paedophiles, rapists, murderers, cruel dictators, serial killers, drug dealers, child abusers and so on. The locusts also represent the evil in all of us.

Sometimes we are shocked by how evil some people can be. We hear of a man who held his daughter captive for twenty-four years in a concealed part of the basement of his family home. He physically assaulted, sexually abused and raped her numerous times during her imprisonment. The incestuous relationship resulted in the birth of seven children and a miscarriage. He kept three of the seven captive underground so they had never seen sunlight.

Or we read of a man and a woman who murdered five children between the ages of ten and seventeen in the Greater Manchester area in the 1960s and are disgusted that as these children were dying, the couple recorded them.

Sometimes there are periods in history when it has been 'exactly as if all hell had been let loose'. It is as if the bottomless pit has been opened by the angel so that the stench of hell comes up and covers a whole nation, or even the whole world. There are periods when sin and vice and immorality are rampant. Day after day the newspapers are full of horrible foul things and vileness and crime are everywhere. All of this evil is the work of these hellish locusts in the hearts of the wicked.

The locusts torment people for five months (Revelation 8:5), which is probably the life span of these creatures. Even though five months can seem like a long time, it is still of limited duration. At the moment we are surrounded by evil but one day God will bring it to an end; it will not go on for ever.

Sixth trumpet

The sixth trumpet is sounded in Revelation 9:13-21. This trumpet is worse than the fifth because the powers of darkness here seem to change men into devils. The sixth trumpet describes war; not a particular war but all wars, especially the most terrifying ones that will happen just before the end of the world. During wars, especially these wars, men will become like devils. Think about Hitler in the Second World War. He instigated numerous violent acts including the systematic murder of an estimated six million Jews.

All wars are warnings for unbelievers.

Four angels with a vast army of vicious horsemen are let loose to kill a third of mankind. The four angels here are different from the four angels in Revelation 7:1; the angels here relish the idea of plunging mankind into war. John sees many horsemen and their riders on the battlefield (9:16-19): two hundred million, which is a symbolic number to signify an enormous crowd.

The riders are all the armies that have ever gone to war, while the horses are no ordinary horses but war engines of every description: tanks, bombs, guns, nuclear weapons etc.

The general meaning of these trumpets is clear. Throughout the whole of history from the first coming of Christ to his second coming, Christ will afflict the enemies of the gospel with disasters, both physical and spiritual. He does this in response to the prayers of the martyrs who cry out for his great name to be vindicated and for all people to repent and turn to him. However, the vast majority of people who hear these warning trumpets remain impenitent. They will not give up their sin and turn to a merciful God (9:20-21). According to Matthew Henry: 'Men who escape these plagues, repent not of their evil works, but go on with idolatries, wickedness, and cruelty, until wrath comes upon them to the utmost.'

AN INTERLUDE — THE CHURCH DURING THESE TRUMPET BLASTS (REVELATION 10:1 - 11:14)

An angel (10:1-3)

In order to announce the seventh trumpet, which is the final judgement, another angel appears (10:1-3). John sees him coming down from heaven; which probably means that John is now on earth. From the beginning of chapter 4 until the end of chapter 9 he has been writing from the perspective of heaven.

The angel he sees is a giant. He is robed in a cloud, with a rainbow above his head. His face is like the sun and his legs are like fiery pillars. His legs are so immense that his left foot rests on the earth while the right one is in the sea. This angel bears similarities to the Lord Jesus Christ, but it is not him. Nowhere in the book of Revelation is the Lord Jesus Christ referred to as an angel; and this being is not worshipped. However, there is a close connection between this angel and Christ. The angel is clearly important and shows the glory of God. The angel's face symbolizes God's holiness. His judgement is indicated by the cloud, while the rainbow portrays his mercy and covenant faithfulness.

In the middle of all these judgements and warnings, God is still merciful and faithful to the covenant he made with all his people. This covenant is the agreement, or promise, that God entered into with sinners who will trust him. If they turn away from their sin and put their faith in Jesus Christ, he will be their God. He will save them, look after them, protect them, love them and give them eternal life in heaven. He has promised this! It shows that God is merciful. God's mercy expresses his goodness and love for the guilty. Remember, this mercy is free. By it we see that God is compassionate, gentle and takes pity on us. He does not treat us as our sins deserve.

A scroll (10:4-11)

In the angel's hand there is an open scroll, and he gives a shout like the roar of a lion. It is clear that the message he has is intended for the entire universe (10:2-3). When the angel shouted, the voices of seven thunders spoke. When the seven thunders spoke, John was about to write down the message but a voice from heaven said, 'Seal up what the seven thunders have said and do not write it down' (10:4, NIV).

There has been much speculation as to what the thunders said, but we simply do not know. John was given a message that he was not to pass on to others in a similar way to Paul in 2 Corinthians 12:4. It is a reminder that there is much more to these huge, eternal issues than we can possibly imagine and fully understand. God has kept some things back from us and we should take this as a warning against thinking we know it all. It should prevent us over-speculating and reading too much into some of the symbols and images in this book. We are mere human beings and God is God.

All we need to know is that the eternal God who created the heavens will accomplish his purposes (10:6-7). Just as he was totally in control at the beginning when he spoke a universe into being, so he will be totally in control in bringing this world to an end. There are things we will never fully understand or be able to get our tiny minds around. We simply must, as Luther said, let God be God.

John is told by the voice from heaven to take the scroll and eat it. When he takes it from the angel he is told that it will taste as sweet as honey but will make his stomach bitter. This means that John, like every true Christian, must experience the sweetness and suffering of the gospel.

When the church faithfully preaches the gospel it will suffer. As we know, John was suffering at that very time. He was on the island of Patmos because of his faith in Jesus Christ. He was writing to people who were really going through it because they were Christians. This has been the testimony of all Christians throughout the centuries to a greater or lesser degree.

Two women aged twenty-seven and thirty were arrested on 5 March 2009 in Tehran and were held in solitary confinement in cramped cells in Evin prison because both were witnessing Christians from a Muslim background. The two really suffered: at first they were held together in very crowded conditions with twenty-seven others, and then in solitary confinement in two metre by two metre cells. They both had serious infections and were interrogated. They stood trial before the revolutionary court without legal representation. Despite all this their faith in Christ did not waver. One said, 'I've taken up my cross, I now have to bear it.'

But this bitterness does not compare with the sweetness of the gospel. To know all your sins forgiven, peace with God and an eternal home in heaven is worth suffering for.

A man became a Christian who had previously been 'one of the boys'. He worked in a garage with other typical lads. When he told the boys he worked with that he had become a Christian they laughed at him and said he would never be able to keep it up and that he would soon be swearing and laughing at dirty jokes and looking at the magazines he used to. One day they grabbed hold of him and pinned him down. Two held his legs and two held his arms while the others got a dirty magazine and put it in front of his eyes. He closed his eyes tight. Afterwards, he was asked what he was thinking of as all of this was going on. He said he was thanking God that he was able to suffer a little for the one who had suffered so much for him.

John is told that he must proclaim this message to peoples, nations, languages and kings (10:11).

Measure the temple of God (11:1-2)

At the beginning of Revelation 11 John is given a measuring rod and told to measure the temple of God and the altar, and count the worshippers there, but to exclude the outer court (Revelation 11:1-2). The church is measured to show that it will be protected during these judgements. It will be protected spiritually but not physically; that is, the church will suffer persecution even to the point of death but their eternal souls will be safe. There will be many martyrs but the church will not be destroyed. In one of his hymns, Martin Luther says,

> And though they take our life,
> Goods, honour, children, wife,
> Yet is their profit small:
> These things shall vanish all:
> The city of God remaineth.

Forty-two months (11:2)

God's people will be trampled on for forty-two months. This is the same length of time as 1,260 days or 3½ years. It corresponds to 'a time, times and half a time' — 'a time' = one year, 'times' = two years and 'half a time' = six months (*cf.* Revelation 12:6,14; 13:5; Daniel 7:25; 12:7). In Revelation 11 it is the period of time the two witnesses prophesy. We will see that in Revelation 12 it is the period of time the woman stays in the wilderness; and in Revelation 13 it is the length of time that the beast exercises his power. In the book of Daniel this period refers to the time when the Jews would suffer between 167–164 BC at the hands of Antiochus Epiphanes. The temple was desecrated, and it was one of the worst times of suffering the Jews endured before God gave them rest again. In Revelation, this length of time is a symbol of the gospel age, from Christ's ascension to heaven to the time just before he returns to this world.

The readers of this Revelation would have discerned that their trial would not go on for ever but would be for a definite period of time. They would one day be delivered. God's people will suffer persecution in this world, but it will only be for a short time in comparison to eternal rest.

The altar (11:1)

It is also significant that John is told to measure the altar. In the Old Testament only the priests were allowed to enter the Holy of Holies where the altar was, but now all believers are allowed to enter in. This shows that all who trust in Jesus Christ can have immediate access to God. When Jesus died on the cross the veil in the temple was rent in two (Matthew 27:51). This was to show that we no longer need a priest to intercede for us before God but can come to him directly wherever we are.

Count the worshippers (11:1)

John has to measure the parameters very carefully and is told to count the worshippers. God knows exactly who the real church is, who trusts in him and who doesn't. You can be a churchgoer, a church member, a Sunday school teacher, a youth leader, a deacon, an elder or even a preacher, but this will not save you when the judgements come. Only those trusting in Jesus Christ will be protected.

Churches that do not hold to faith alone, Christ alone, grace alone and Scripture alone will not be saved, however influential, important and worldwide they think they are and appear to be.

The Puritan John Bunyan, in his famous book *Pilgrim's Progress*, which he wrote whilst in prison in 1676, describes the glorious scene at the end of the book when Christian enters heaven. He also describes Ignorance arriving at the gates. Ignorance thought he was a Christian but he wasn't, and on arrival at heaven he is turned away. His hands and feet are bound and he is thrown out. Bunyan comments: 'Then I saw that there was a way to hell even from the gates of heaven.' The same is true of every church and chapel; every Christian camp, conference and youth group. There is a way to hell from every one of them.

Two witnesses (11:3-12)

During the time that the people of God will be trampled on, two witnesses are appointed by God to prophesy clothed in sackcloth (11:3). The witnesses are clothed in sackcloth because their message is that people should repent, and in the Old Testament people put on sackcloth and put ashes on their heads to show they were repentant.

These two witnesses are a collective symbol of the church. When Jesus Christ sent his disciples out preaching the gospel he sent them out two by two, and in the Old Testament two witnesses were needed to give competent legal testimony (Deuteronomy 17:6; 19:15). Every Christian and the church throughout the ages have a duty to proclaim the gospel of repentance and faith to a hostile world.

The two witnesses are identified as two olive trees and two lampstands (11:4). They are identified like this because the church is constantly supplied with the oil of the Holy Spirit and shows light to a dark world, like a lampstand. It reveals the truth to a world that is being deceived, showing them things as they really are. Christians on their own cannot persuade anyone to turn to Christ. We are totally reliant on the Holy Spirit. Only he can change a person's heart, convince them of their sin and show them the Saviour.

However, the gospel age will one day come to an end (*cf.* Matthew 24:14). Today churches and missionary organizations preach the gospel worldwide. But one day, just before the end, even though there will be a few believers left on the earth (Luke 18:8), the testimony of the church as a whole will end.

Revelation 11:7 says that the beast, which is the antichristian world, urged on by hell, will battle against the church and kill it. Not all Christians will be destroyed, but there will be increasing opposition just before the end. It will be a time of humiliation for the church (11:8-10). The world will be glad to see the back of her and the uncomfortable preaching about repentance. But it will be for a very short time, only three and a half days compared to three and a half months of the church's ministry. It will be Satan's little season, his last furore.

After this very short period, the church will rise again. The two witnesses, the church, hear a loud voice from heaven. The voice says, 'Come up here!' 'And they went up to heaven in a cloud while their enemies looked on' (11:12, NIV).

But the hour of victory for the church is the hour of judgement for the world (11:13). In this verse John only describes the first shock of the final catastrophe to stress the terrified reaction of the rest of humanity.

The phrase at the end of verse 13, 'and the rest were terrified and gave glory to the God of heaven' (ESV), causes disagreement between Bible scholars. Some believe that at the very end the unbelievers who were not destroyed by the earthquake were sorry and repented, and God in his grace forgave them. However, it seems more likely that this was not real repentance but remorse for the plight they were in. Genuine conversion is no longer possible. As long as the Word is proclaimed there is time for salvation; but now that the witnesses have already ascended to heaven, it is too late for people to repent. What a sobering thought! One day it will be too late. Today is a day of grace. You can call on Jesus Christ now and he will save you, whoever you are and whatever you've done. But one day the day of grace will be over. You will call to him then and he will not hear you. That day might be tomorrow. Only today is the day of salvation.

One thing is sure; those who oppose the gospel will eventually bring judgement upon themselves (vv. 5-6).

However, before this final end, the world will often rejoice over the death of the church, only to see it rise again (11:11). There have been many times in the history of the world when the church has appeared to be down and out and an absolute irrelevance. The world laughed at it and thought it has outgrown it, only for it to rise again.

This happens during times when God revives his church. People are saved and the community as a whole is affected and transformed. This was the case in England in the eighteenth century. According to Dallimore, life in England between 1730 and 1740 was foul with moral corruption and crippled by spiritual decay, very similar to the condition of the west in our day and age. As today, people thought the church had had its day. Sin was too rampant. But during this dark time, 'England was startled by the sound of a voice' (Dallimore, *George Whitefield*, p.31). It was the voice of the preacher George Whitefield. God used this voice and others, including John and Charles Wesley, to make his church rise again. Wouldn't it be amazing if in these days we were startled again by the sound of a voice!

THE SEVENTH TRUMPET — REVELATION 11:15-19

In Revelation 11:14 there is the announcement of the third woe, the seventh trumpet (11:14). This is the final judgement; but instead of focusing on the terror of that day, John pictures something greater, a scene in heaven after the judgement (11:15-19). While the unbelievers face torment, God's people enjoy intimate fellowship with him. God's temple is open and the Ark of the Covenant is there (11:19). In the Old Testament the Ark of the Covenant was a symbol of God's presence with his people. Now there is nothing hidden: everything is revealed. There are no barriers between God and his people. They are blissfully happy and safe for ever in his company.

SECOND DIVISION

SECTION 4

The woman and the child persecuted

by the dragon and his helpers

(Revelation 12 - 14)

10

THE WOMAN, THE CHILD AND THE DRAGON

Revelation 12

Chapter 12 marks a new division in the book of Revelation. The first division (chapters 1 - 11) focuses on the struggle among people; between believers and unbelievers. The world attacks the church but the church is avenged, protected and victorious.

The second division (chapters 12 - 22) reveals that the struggle on earth has a deeper background. It shows us why unbelievers hate believers so vehemently and what will happen at the end of the world. It takes us behind the scenes.

THE CHURCH'S BIGGEST PROBLEM

What causes the church its greatest problems? What do Christians struggle with most? If you are a Christian what would you say your biggest difficulty is?

Some of the first readers of this book would say persecution. Most were being bitterly persecuted. Their blood was being poured out

(6:10; 16:6; 17:6; 19:2); some were pining away in dingy dungeons while others were about to be imprisoned (2:10); some were suffering from hunger, thirst and famine (6:8; 7:16); some of the Christians had been cast before wild beasts (6:8); some had been beheaded (20:4).

Others would say the biggest problem was false teachers and sects that were troubling the church (2:2, 14, 20, 24).

Others might say false religion (13:7, 15; 17:18).

They would all confess that they struggle with sin and temptation of various kinds.

What about Christians today? Maybe you would say the attraction of the world; being left out and not being part of the crowd. Perhaps there are particular temptations you face or sins you really struggle with. There could be a particular person who is giving you a hard time because you are a Christian.

You may look at the state of the church today and conclude that the biggest problem the church faces is that she seems marginalized in society, misunderstood and mistreated by the world. You may feel that your own church's attempts to evangelize and reach people are ineffective. Maybe your church has suffered a split with people leaving to start up their own church or join another.

All of these struggles are all very real and cause the church great distress. But none of these are the church's biggest problem. The church's biggest problem is the rage of Satan! According to Dr D. Martyn Lloyd-Jones:

> *We all know something about persecution. We know what it is to be confronted by people who are unbelievers and anti-Christian, and how difficult they can make life for us at times.*

Yes, we know all that, but that is not the whole story. We need to be made aware of the fact that these men and women, these individuals, are but instruments of the great powers behind our world. The Bible impresses upon us the truth that it is the devil who is fighting God. So often we fail to remember that and, therefore, become confused and cannot understand things. What you and I see with our physical eyes is simply the visible part of a great spiritual war that is going on in another realm, in which we are being used, as it were, as the instruments

(The Church and the Last Things, p.176).

THE WOMAN, THE CHILD AND THE DRAGON (12:1-6)

At the beginning of Revelation 12 John sees a woman about to give birth. As she does so, in front of her stands a dragon ready to devour the child.

The picture is grotesque. But what does it mean? Who is the woman? Who is the child? Who is the dragon?

The woman

The woman is the church (*cf.* 12:17). The description of her in verse 1 emphasizes the dignity of her position. There is a glaring contrast between the heavenly glory of the woman and the earthly glitter of the great harlot described in 17:4.

The child

The woman is pregnant and cries in agony as she labours to give birth to her child. The child is Jesus and has been a long time coming. He has been promised since the very beginning, from the moment Adam and Eve fell (Genesis 3:15; Micah 5:2-3). The whole of the Old Testament looks forward and anticipates the coming of this child.

The dragon

The dragon is Satan. He is a red dragon because he is intent on murder. He is determined to kill the child. His ten horns symbolize the completeness of his power over all the earth. His seven crowns signify his arrogated authority.

His tail swept a third of the stars out of the sky and flung them to the earth (12:4). He causes a third of the universe to collapse. His actions are catastrophic; he is bent on devastation and destruction and will do whatever it takes to destroy the child, the Lord Jesus Christ. This is clearly seen when Christ is born. Herod, an instrument in the hand of Satan, decrees that every baby under two years old should be killed in a desperate attempt to kill the Lord Jesus (Matthew 2:16).

The son to whom the woman gives birth will rule all the nations. Her child was snatched up to God and to his throne, showing that Satan fails to destroy the Lord Jesus Christ. This refers to the Lord Jesus Christ's ascension back to heaven. This is not dealt with in much detail because the focus of the chapter is not on the child but on the woman.

The wilderness

After the child ascended to heaven the woman fled to the wilderness, a place prepared for her by God. The desert was the place where God's people in the Old Testament wandered for forty years after they came out of slavery in Egypt and before they entered the Promised Land. It was a place of testing, but also a place where God miraculously provided for his people and wooed them. In the desert the people were completely dependent on God to be their provider and protector.

The woman is in the wilderness for 1,260 days (see section on 'forty-two months' in chapter 9, p.95). She will be in the wilderness for this definite, fixed period but will be brought by God into the Promised Land.

This pictures the experience of the church throughout history. This world is like a wilderness and the church will encounter many trials and difficulties; but God will provide for her, and one day the people of God will enter heaven for ever.

THE WAR IN HEAVEN (12:7-10)

Revelation 12:7-10 records a war in heaven between Michael and his angels and the dragon and his angels. The dragon and his angels lost and were thrown out of heaven.

Even though the devil was thrown out of heaven before the world was made, he was defeated once and for all when Christ died on Calvary. In Luke 10 the Lord Jesus Christ said, 'I saw Satan fall from heaven.' This actually happened when the Lord Jesus Christ died on the cross and rose again. In former times Satan could enter heaven as the accuser of God's people (Job 1:6-12; Zechariah 3:1-2); but now that the price of their redemption has been paid, he can no longer do so (Romans 8:34).

Michael is one of the archangels. He is mentioned in the Old Testament as a prince and protector of God's people (Daniel 10:13, 21; 12:1). He is represented as the victor of the war in heaven. He is like the staff officer who is able to remove Satan's flag from the heavenly map because the officer in the field has won the real victory on Calvary.

Even though the dragon has been defeated he will not be cast into hell until the very end of time. He knows he is defeated, but is determined to cause as much havoc as possible before he is finally cast into hell.

One of the things the devil does is to torment Christians. He is called 'the accuser of the brethren'. He reminds people of their sin and whispers to them that there is no way they can be right with God. He brings to their memory all their failures and haunts them with their past. But after Christ's victory on Calvary his accusations lose every semblance of justice.

As the hymn-writer Charitie Lees Bancroft puts it:

When Satan tempts me to despair
And tells me of the guilt within,
Upward I look, and see Him there
Who made an end of all my sin.

The dragon pursuing the woman (12:13-17)

Since the moment Satan was thrown out of heaven, his power has been restricted. He no longer has access to God. He realizes that he now has no chance of overcoming the child so he turns all of his vengeance on the woman. He is wicked and frustrated. He is filled with rage because he knows his time is short and so he aims to do as much damage as possible. He knows his success is limited but will do whatever he can to wreak havoc.

He pursues the woman in the wilderness, but God protects her.

Throughout this life every Christian experiences Satan persecuting and troubling them but God helping and protecting them.

The way Christians overcome this satanic rage (12:11)

Revelation 12:11 gives three ways that Christians can overcome the rage of Satan.

Firstly, they overcame him by the blood of the Lamb. When the devil accuses us and makes us feel guilty, we'll never beat him by saying, 'I'm not that bad.' The only way we can ever beat Satan is on the grounds of the blood of the Lamb. As Christians we can have good days and bad days; days we feel like Christians and days we don't. Days we really fail him and days we feel close to God. But our feelings are not what save us. The only way to overcome accusations is on the grounds of the blood of the Lamb.

One day I will stand before God. There will be many people who know me who could present a case as to why I should not be allowed into heaven. People I grew up with, went to school with, went to university with, worked with, my family, friends: all could point to my sins and say that there's no way he should be allowed into heaven. Then there is my conscience that can bring to mind the things I've thought and done that no one else knows. That will definitely condemn me! On top of all that, God's law shows me I've failed at every point. The devil will accuse me through all of these things. But on that awesome day when I stand before the Judge of all the earth, Jesus Christ will plead for me. He will stand with me and when the devil, the law, my conscience, my past and everyone who knows me will condemn me, he will say, as it were, 'Look back to before the sun, the moon and all the stars were made; that is when I set my love upon you. Look at those three crosses. On the middle one, I took all your sins upon myself and paid for every one of them! When you confessed your sins to me I was faithful and just and forgave you. When you called upon me I saved you. My blood covers all your iniquities.'

Don't look at yourself; trust in the blood of the Lamb! Say with Horatius Bonar,

> Upon a life I did not live,
> Upon a death I did not die;
> Another's life, another's death,
> I stake my whole eternity.

Secondly, they overcame him by the word of their testimony. How do we fight the devil and attempt to transform society by the gospel? By the word of our testimony. As Christians we will never beat the world by trying to be like the world. We'll never win people for the gospel by trying to be cool or trendy. God has promised to bless just two things: prayer and preaching. Never lose faith in them! To give one example: in Cardiff in the 1970s, 80s and early 90s, a frail man stood in a pulpit. He preached from a seventeenth-century Bible and sang hymns that were mainly from the eighteenth century. Hundreds were won for the gospel. His secret was his unflinching faith in preaching and prayer and an absolute dependence on the Holy Spirit.

Thirdly, they were willing to die. A Christian realizes that death has lost its sting. The apostle Paul said, 'For to me to live is Christ and to die is gain' (Phil. 1:21, ESV). For Christians, death means to be with God, so it holds no fear for them. Witnesses say that the Christian martyrs embraced the flames like a stream on a hot summer's day. As he was about to die, William Haslam said, 'I am just beginning to live.'

This chapter shows us that behind all the enemies of the church, which come in a variety of forms, is Satan himself. The only way the church and individual believers overcome Satan is by the blood of the Lamb, the word of their testimony and by not loving their lives even unto death (12:11).

11

THE BEAST OF THE SEA
AND THE BEAST OF THE EARTH

Revelation 13

INTRODUCTION

At the beginning of chapter 13 the dragon of chapter 12 is standing where the land and the sea meet. He is at the seashore in order to summon help. A beast comes out of the sea and a beast comes out of the earth.

The first — the beast of the sea — is a monster of indescribable horror. The second — the beast of the earth — has the appearance of being harmless, and for that reason is more dangerous. The first monster is what Satan does; the second is how he thinks.

A third helper of Satan is mentioned in the next chapter — the harlot Babylon (Revelation 14:8). These three helpers comprise antichristian persecution, antichristian religion and wisdom, and antichristian seduction.

THE BEAST OF THE SEA (REVELATION 13:1-10)

The dragon gives the beast its power and authority. The sea represents the nations and governments of the world. The beast of the sea is the persecuting power of Satan embodied in all the nations and governments of the world throughout history. The beast of the sea represents the persecution of Christians.

The beast of the sea had seven heads with ten horns covered with crowns. On each head is a blasphemous name (13:1). He had the body of a leopard, the feet of a bear and the mouth of a lion (13:2). A leopard is large and fierce and springs swiftly upon its prey, while a bear is ready to rend and tear and use its terrible feet to crush its enemy. His lion's mouth would growl and roar. The image is horrific!

The beast has seven heads, which signifies that the beast assumes different forms. At one period in history it could be Rome, while at another time it is Babylon, and so on.

One of the beast's heads seemed to be mortally wounded, but the fatal wound had been healed (13:3). This is probably referring to Nero. He was the Roman emperor between AD 54 and 68 and was a monster of wickedness. He clearly illustrates this antichristian persecution. A fire broke out in Rome and (rightly or wrongly) Nero was suspected of deliberately causing the fire. To divert the blame from himself he blamed the Christians. According to the Roman historian Tacitus:

> *Nero punished with the utmost refinement of cruelty a class hated for their abominations who are commonly called Christians. In Rome an immense multitude was convicted, not so much on the charge of arson as because of their hatred*

of the human race. Besides being put to death they were made to serve as objects of amusement; they were clad in the hides of beasts and torn to pieces by dogs; others were crucified, others set on fire to serve to illuminate the night when daylight failed (Houghton, *Sketches from Church History,* p.10).

In AD 68 Nero committed suicide and it looked as if the persecution was over — it had received a mortal wound. But under the new emperor, Domitian, persecution resumed; hence the head that was healed. The beast has ten horns and history shows that even though different countries and empires rise and fall, behind them all is the beast of the sea — antichristian persecution.

The world hates Jesus Christ. Maybe you are not sure you believe that. You think that the world is indifferent to him or is not particularly interested in him, but would not go as far as to say that it hates him. But the fact that the Western world does not seem bothered by Jesus Christ has got everything to do with the church's witness in these days. The church doesn't seem that different from the world at the moment, so why would the world hate the church and her Lord and Saviour? However, when Christians live as they should and preach the true gospel clearly and faithfully, it is bound to offend the world and lead to persecution.

The church's message is that all have sinned. People hate to be told that they are sinners. There are sins the Bible condemns and commands people to repent of which would cut across many people's lifestyles and life choices. The church's message is that unless people repent of their sins they will spend an eternity in hell. The only way a person can be saved is by trusting in Jesus Christ. He is the only way to get to God and go to heaven; all other religions are false. If the church preaches these truths and lives out these beliefs, she will face persecution.

Above all, Jesus Christ told people that they had to deny themselves if they were to follow him (Matthew 16:24). They have to give up living for themselves and doing what they like. They now have to seek to please and honour God. People hate being told to deny themselves. We all love ourselves and want to please ourselves. But the church's message is that we are answerable to the one who made us and our chief aim must be to glorify God.

Even though this world hates the church and will persecute it, Christians should not go out of their way to be offensive and condemning; certainly never self-righteous! We should be as kind, winsome, loving and sociable as we can be, always remembering that we have been saved by grace and there is nothing in and of ourselves that has merited the love of God. By nature we are all the same.

The Bible says that Jesus grew in favour with all men. He loved people and was moved with compassion when he saw the crowds. We should be like him.

It is our message that offends. We should never apologize for it or dilute it.

The beast is given power to make war against the saints and to conquer them. He has authority over every tribe, people, language and nation. All the inhabitants of the world whose names are not written in the Lamb's book of life worship the beast (13:7-8).

The beast has authority for forty-two months, again linking to the prophecy in the book of Daniel concerning the time the Jews suffered at the hands of Antiochus Epiphanes. It was one of the worst times of suffering the Jews endured; but it did not last for ever.

This antichristian persecution which seems to rule and be in control will not last for ever. One day God will give his people eternal rest. However, in the meantime there is a need for patient endurance and faithfulness on the part of the saints (13:10). If you are suffering as a Christian in whatever way, be patient and remain faithful. One day it will be over. The hymn-writer James Grindlay Small says,

The eternal glories gleam afar
To nerve my faint endeavour:
So now to watch! to work! to war!
And then — to rest for ever.

Being a Christian can be difficult. There will be times when you will wonder whether it is worth it and will want to give up; but remember heaven, 'the glories that gleam afar', and remember the end of all those who now reject Jesus Christ and persecute his church.

Daley Thompson was a gold medallist in the decathlon at the Los Angeles Olympics in 1984. As I am sure you know, the decathlon is made up of ten events, track and field. The last event is the 1500 metres. After he won the gold medal, an interviewer asked Thompson how he felt about having to run the 1500 metres after having done nine events. He replied: 'I thought about the gold medal and told myself, "Whatever it takes!"' When persecution comes and the going gets tough, and you are about to give up, think about the prize and tell yourself, 'Whatever it takes.'

THE BEAST OF THE EARTH (13:11-18)

This beast looked very different. It had two little horns just like a lamb. It looked like a pet for children. But it speaks like a dragon! It is false religion and the wisdom of this world. It seems so harmless and what it says seems to make such sense, but it is the lie of Satan dressed up as the truth.

This beast of the earth fully cooperates with the beast of the sea. This beast is able to perform great and miraculous signs (13:13) and deceive the inhabitants of the earth (13:14).

In the ancient world statues were regarded as the natural means by which the gods could have intercourse with their worshippers and the priests of the day had the trick of making the statues speak. Mounce records:

> *Belief in statues which spoke and performed miracles is widely attested in ancient literature. Simon Magus is reported to have brought statues to life ... it was the age of Apollonius of Tyana, whose trickery was held to come from the powers of evil. Ventriloquism was practised by the priests of Oriental cults, and sorcery had found a place in the official circles of Rome*
> *(Revelation, p.258).*

Religious charlatans are able to perform seeming miracles. This has been true since the very beginning. In the Old Testament, God's prophets performed miracles to show that their message was authentic and from God. However, false prophets imitated the miracles of the true prophets to deceive the people into worshipping false gods. Deuteronomy 13:1 warns of false prophets who would lead people to worship other gods by means of signs and wonders. In John's day they could apparently bring fire down from heaven to persuade people to worship the emperor's image (13:14-15). Jesus predicted the rise of false christs who would lead astray, if possible, even the very elect (Mark 13:22).

When the Antichrist comes, his appearance will be marked out by numerous miracles. The second beast carries out his task of deception in fulfilment of these expectations. Even though God alone can perform a true miracle, we should never underestimate the power and skill and subtlety of the devil.

Today there are people who seem to perform amazing signs and wonders: spiritualists, fortune-tellers and the like. There are even people who are so-called Christians who do seeming miracles and get many people to follow them. But their powers are not from God. It is frightening to think that things done in the name of Jesus Christ may actually be the work of the devil himself. According to Luther, 'the devil cannot peddle his lies unless he adorns them with the beloved name'. It is important to test everything by the Word of God. Just because something happens in a church or in the name of Christ does not mean it is real. The devil has powers and will use them to deceive whoever he can.

Not only does the beast of the earth do wonders to make people follow the beast of the sea, but he deceives people into accepting what is spoken by Satan as the truth. He does this through false religion and the wisdom of this world.

The wisdom of this world makes God's Word, the Bible, seem outdated and ludicrous. One of the most obvious ways it does this is by convincing people that anyone who believes in God is committing intellectual suicide. This belief is perhaps most aggressively presented these days in the bestselling book by Richard Dawkins (*The God Delusion*), where he argues that anyone who believes there is a God is deluded. On the inside cover of the book, Matt Ridley says that the book is a 'resounding trumpet blast for truth'. The book clearly shows, though, that it's not so much that Dawkins doesn't believe in God; he hates him. As George Orwell would say, 'He was an embittered atheist, the sort of atheist who does not so much disbelieve in God as personally dislike him.' You cannot not believe in God and hate him at the same time. Everyone deep down believes in God. 'By night an Atheist half believes in a God' (Young, *The Complaint*, p.98). More importantly, in the first chapter of Romans, the apostle Paul says that God has made himself known to everyone; but people have chosen to exchange the truth of God for a lie. This 'uncertainty' by those who maintain that there 'certainly' is no God was evident in the atheist bus campaign promoted by the *Guardian* newspaper and supported by Richard Dawkins. The slogan on the buses read: 'There's *probably* no God. Now stop worrying and enjoy your life.'

People will believe anything if it means they don't have to believe in a God to whom they are answerable: to the point that people convince themselves that in the beginning there was a big bang and from that big bang this universe came into being. Then over billions of years, life evolved. This theory maintains that the chair you are sitting on reading this book, or the bed you are lying on, has more purpose in life than you do, because they were made for a reason — for you to lie or sit on — but you are just an accident.

Imagine going to buy a new car. You look around the showroom and the salesman points out all the different cars. He shows you one and says what a great car it is and how you can always trust Volkswagen to make good cars. He then takes you to a BMW and tells you what fine car makers they are. On you go to an Audi and the same is true of those cars, very well made. Then you come to another car and he says that this one is a funny one because it hasn't got a maker. They were in the office one day and heard a big bang and then over the next few days, weeks and months the car began to evolve; first a steering wheel, then seats, followed by electric windows, a gear box, the engine and so on. You'd think it was nuts! And yet so many look at the Grand Canyon, the Niagara Falls, the oceans and seas, the mountain ranges, the stars and planets, and tell themselves it just happened! Blanchard says, 'If the brain is nothing more than an accident of biological evolution, why should we trust its ability to tell us so? How can chance accumulations of atoms and molecules decide that that is what they are?' (*Evolution: Fact or Fiction*, p.30).

An example of human wisdom wanting to explain God away was found in *The Week* (2 October 2010). Some scientists in America now accept that the parting of the Red Sea could have happened. However, they explain it by saying that having estimated the depth of the water three thousand years ago at six feet, a 63mph east wind blowing for twelve hours could have driven the water back on both sides of the bend, creating a three-mile-wide, two-mile-long land bridge. As soon as the wind died down, the water would have rushed back. If that was the case, the timing of it all is almost as incredible as the sea parting! To think that the waters were driven back at the right time to let the Israelites go through and then the wind died down at the moment Pharaoh's armies tried to go through the water! Isn't it more believable that an almighty God parted the sea and controlled the whole event?

Furthermore, the beast of the earth deludes people into thinking there is no God by making them sceptical and putting questions in their mind like: 'Why does God allow suffering in the world?'; 'How could a loving God send people to hell?'; 'How can one religion be right and the others wrong?' Instead of looking for the answers to these questions in the Bible, people choose to believe the wisdom of the world.

The beast of the earth also expresses itself in all the false religions and sects of the world. Many of these religions seem to say commendable, worthy things. They seem harmless. But they all have the same problem. They are all man-made. They are all about man's attempts to get right with God. Some advocate that to have your sins forgiven you must wash in a particular river; others say you have to stop eating during daylight for one month every year, or go on a journey to a holy place; others say that you need to confess your sins to a priest and do penance, and so on. Every one of them is about a person's efforts to get to God.

Christianity says you can do nothing. There is no way you can please God. It is faith alone in Christ alone. Come to Jesus Christ just as you are and simply trust in his finished work at Golgotha on your behalf.

Not only are there false religions. There is also a false Christianity. It tries to make itself more palatable and acceptable to the world. It takes out all the bits which people don't like — some of God's laws, hell, etc. It also takes out the bits people find hard to believe — the supernatural. The logic is that any story in the Bible which my tiny little mind cannot comprehend simply cannot be true and so must be taken out. We are therefore left with a weak and pathetic Christianity which doesn't offend but does not really say anything either.

But maybe the cleverest tactic of the beast of the earth is the one described by Lewis in *The Screwtape Letters*. He imagines a discussion between the devil and junior devils. The devil asks the junior devils to come up with ways they can stop people becoming Christians. One suggests telling people there is no God; but that is dismissed because everyone believes there is a God. Next they suggest telling people there is no heaven or hell; but again, deep down people believe there are. One of the devils suggests that they tell people that there is a God and a heaven and a hell, and they do need to be saved. But also tell them there is no hurry! Maybe that is the devil's lie that you are believing as you read this book. All these things are true and one day you need to do business with God; but there's no hurry.

You cannot afford to take any chances with your never dying soul. A story is told of a man who sold everything he had to buy a precious diamond. He was on the deck of a ship one day, tossing the diamond up in the air and catching it, tossing it up in the air and catching it. A lady approached him and told him how foolish he was being and how he needed to take care of something so precious. He laughed and told her to stop worrying; that he had been doing it for ages and it was fine. He threw the diamond up again — but suddenly the boat jerked and the diamond fell into the water. The man screamed at the top of his voice, 'Lost! Lost! Everything is lost!' Maybe you are playing with your soul. You've been doing it for ages and it's fine. But God will suddenly say that your soul is required of you and you'll spend eternity screaming, 'Lost! Lost! Everything is lost!'

THE MARK OF THE BEAST (13:16-17)

In order to show their loyalty to the beast, everyone is forced to have the mark of the beast (13:16). Those who do not have this mark cannot buy or sell. Today, Christians who refuse to conform to the world suffer. An obvious example of this would be a sportsperson who refuses to play on a Sunday. He or she would miss out on important matches and probably would not be offered a contract because so many matches are played on a Sunday.

The mark of the beast is 666. Slaves were branded or marked to show that they belonged to their master. The followers of the Lamb are sealed on their foreheads to show that they belong to him. The mark of the beast is symbolic. Seven is the number of perfection. The number which represents man is six, because he was created on the sixth day. Despite all his efforts man can never attain perfection. He never becomes seven. The mark of man who does not belong to the Lamb is 666. According to Hendriksen: 'The number of the beast is 666, that is, failure upon failure upon failure!' (*More Than Conquerors*, p.151).

12

SONGS OF JOY
AND WARNINGS OF JUDGEMENT

Revelation 14

THE LAMB AND THE 144,000 ON MOUNT ZION
(REVELATION 14:1-5)

In chapter 13 John sees the dragon enlisting the help of the beast of the sea and the beast of the earth. The chapter describes this world with its antichristian governments and false religion persecuting the church and deceiving the vast majority of people. It is a painful yet all too real picture for Christians.

But at the beginning of chapter 14 John sees something wonderful. He says, 'Then I looked, and behold a Lamb standing on Mount Zion, and with him one hundred and forty-four thousand having his Father's name written on their foreheads' (14:1, NKJV).

In verse 3 they are singing a song which no one else could sing. In verse 4 it says they had not defiled themselves and were like virgins. Verse 5 says that there was no deceit in their mouths and they were without fault before the throne of God.

Who are this great multitude? They are saved sinners. They were by nature and practice like everyone else: rotten, filthy, hell-deserving sinners; but they have been made clean by the Lord Jesus Christ. In 1 Corinthians 6:9-10 (NASB), the apostle Paul says, 'Do you not know that the unrighteous will not inherit the kingdom of God? Do not be deceived: neither fornicators, nor idolaters, nor adulterers, nor effeminate, nor homosexuals, nor thieves, nor the covetous, nor drunkards, nor revilers, nor swindlers, will inherit the kingdom of God.' None of us have got a chance, then! But this multitude at the beginning of chapter 14, undefiled, with no deceit in their mouths and without fault is made up of people just like that. How, you say? Well, in 1 Corinthians 6:11, Paul goes on to say, 'Such were some of you; but you were washed, but you were sanctified, but you were justified in the name of the Lord Jesus Christ and in the Spirit of our God' (NASB). This multitude is full of sinners whom God has made clean.

Rev. Vernon Higham, pastor of Heath Evangelical Church in Cardiff, on more than one occasion referred to a lady who attended the Heath church in the 1980s. She had lived a particularly dirty life but had started attending the Heath church and realized her sinfulness and trusted the Lord Jesus Christ to save her. She would go back to where she was staying with many other women, who would taunt her that someone like her should never be going to church and that with her past she could never be forgiven. She felt hopeless and unclean. But she told Mr Higham that one night after a particularly bad evening, it was as if the Lord Jesus Christ himself drew near to her and said, 'In my sight you are a chaste virgin.'

There is no wonder these people are singing. People sing when they are happy, especially when they are victorious. In 2008 I was at the Millennium Stadium in Cardiff watching Wales beat France to win yet another Grand Slam. Along with the other 70,000 Welsh fans I couldn't help singing! We sang our hearts out! We were so happy, all we could do was sing! I hugged people I didn't even know because we were all so happy! Well, let me multiply that by infinity.

The singing here isn't in response to some measly game involving an egg-shaped ball. The singing here is because hell-deserving people, riddled with sin, have been forgiven and had their sins removed by the work of an Almighty Saviour. They are counted righteous by a holy God. It is overwhelming! They can't believe it. No wonder they are singing! Only those who have experienced such love can sing this song. A friend of mine, when he became a Christian, ran through an open field jumping and punching the air in happiness. He couldn't believe all his sins had been forgiven, his past had been forgotten and that the judge and creator of the whole universe loved him.

These people are blessed and have rest from their labours (14:13). They are happy, have the favour of God upon them, and are at peace.

WARNINGS (REVELATION 14:6-11)

John sees three angels who announce the nearness of the end, the fall of Babylon and the doom of the beast's worshippers. These angels belong together and have one purpose, which is to warn mankind.

The first angel proclaimed the eternal gospel to those who dwell on the earth. It means to those who 'sit on the earth'. The picture is one of an angel proclaiming this gospel with urgency; but the people are sitting down in a very relaxed manner. They are easy-going and indifferent to the message they are hearing. They are too fascinated with this world and all its earthly charms, and completely unaware of their peril. If you are reading this book indifferent to the gospel, or you have friends and family who have no interest in Jesus Christ and are completely unaware of their need to be saved, pray that God would move them by his Spirit. Only the Spirit can alert people to the reality and importance of these things. George Whitefield was a preacher greatly used by God in the eighteenth-century revival. It was said of those who listened to him that they were all attention, and heard like people hearing for eternity.

The second angel (14:8) proclaimed: 'Fallen, fallen is Babylon the great.' Babylon refers to this world and all its pleasures. As hard as it is to imagine, one day this world will come to an end.

The third angel announces with a loud voice that all those who are attached to this world are going to perish with this world. They will drink of the wrath of God and be tormented with fire and brimstone. The smoke of their torment ascends for ever and ever and they have no rest day or night (14:10-11). People who have no time for God but are just completely taken up with this world will perish with this world.

JUDGEMENT DAY (REVELATION 14:14-16)

These verses describe a harvest at the end of the world. It is a picture of judgement day when the Lord Jesus Christ will divide all human beings into two groups. When Christ reaps this harvest everyone will be there. All the important figures from history will be there: Winston Churchill, Martin Luther King, Gandhi, etc. All the sports people of the day — like David Beckham and Usain Bolt — will be there. Influential people such as Simon Cowell and Lord Sugar will be there. World leaders like Barak Obama and David Cameron. Pop stars and movie stars. You'll be there and I'll be there.

All of us, however famous or insignificant, however rich or poor, however educated or uneducated, will be judged by God and divided into two groups. One group will be consigned to everlasting torment in hell and the other will enter eternal paradise in heaven. On that day all that matters will be what you did with Jesus Christ; did you accept him or reject him? There will be some people on that awful day whose shoes I would not want to be in. Imagine being Hitler or Saddam Hussain or another person who has been guilty of heinous crimes, standing before a just God!

But the people who will be the saddest on that day will be those who heard the gospel and were almost persuaded. They read books like this, heard sermons, went to youth groups and on Christian camps and almost put their faith in the Lord Jesus Christ; but something, some person, some fear or some sin, held them back. They will spend eternity regretting it over and over and over again!

ETERNAL PUNISHMENT (REVELATION 14:17-20)

Revelation 14:17-20 describes what happens to the wicked on judgement day. An angel came out of the temple which is in heaven with a sharp sickle. Another angel who has power over fire came out from the altar and called with a loud voice to the one who had the sharp sickle to 'put in your sharp sickle and gather the clusters from the vine of the earth, because her grapes are ripe' (14:15, NASB).

The vine of the earth symbolizes the entire multitude of unbelieving men and women and the grapes are the individual unbelievers. The grapes are cast into the great winepress of the wrath of God and crushed. They are thrown into a lake of blood so deep that horses can swim in it. This lake spreads out in all directions to the extent of 1600 stadia. That is 4x4x10x10. Four is the number of the universe and ten is the number which symbolizes completeness. The image conveys the thoroughly complete judgement of the wicked.

It is a terrifying prospect. The picture here is intended to convey the horrors of hell. The reality is far worse. Everything we enjoy in this life — friendship, good food, a warm summer's evening, crunching through snow — is no longer ours to enjoy.

Hell is a place of absolute pain. We will gnash our teeth; we'll be in torment day and night; we'll be in outer darkness; our consciences will plague us throughout eternity. It is also a place where God is but only in his anger. We will spend eternity in the presence of an angry God. And there is no escape; no fire exit; no prospect of getting out. Dante said that over the gates of hell would be the words, 'Abandon hope, all ye who enter here'.

I went to hospital recently and had to have an endoscopy. It was the worst experience of my life so far! I knew I was in trouble when one person held my arms and another held my legs down! A nurse kept telling me to keep calm as a doctor pushed a tube with a camera on the end of it down my throat. For twenty minutes I retched as with two hands on the tube the doctor pushed and shoved it around my stomach! It was awful. But after twenty minutes it was over.

Hell is torment; but it won't be over after twenty minutes. It won't be over after twenty years. It won't be over after twenty million years. In fact, for those who end up there it won't be over at all!

Heed the warnings and seek the Lord while he may be found. He will save you now. Come to him.

Section 5

Seven bowls

(Revelation 15 - 16)

13

SEVEN BOWLS

Revelation 15 and 16

SUMMARY

Chapters 15 and 16 describe the fifth vision that John saw — the bowls of wrath. These bowls of wrath are closely linked to the seven seals and the seven trumpets. The seals unveil God's judgements and the trumpets warn of his judgements, while the bowls are the actual outpouring of these judgements.

At the beginning of chapter 15 we can almost smell the judgements of God; but before John describes these judgements, he shows us the triumphant church after the last day when all the seven bowls have been poured out. He sees a sea of crystal (15:2-4) and the heavenly temple (15:5-8).

THE SEA OF CRYSTAL (REVELATION 15:2-4)

John sees a sea. On the seashore is a great, victorious multitude, who played their harps and sang the song of Moses. This is reminiscent of Exodus 15. The children of Israel, God's Old Testament people, had been slaves in Egypt. God commanded Pharaoh to let his people go but Pharaoh refused. To make him change his mind, God sent a series of plagues on Egypt, but still Pharaoh would not let the Israelites go. After the tenth plague, the death of the eldest son in every Egyptian family, Pharaoh finally agreed to let them go. However, as soon as they had left Egypt he chased after them to get them back. They were confronted by an impossible situation. They had the Red Sea in front of them and Pharaoh's army behind them. Miraculously, God enabled Moses to part the Red Sea, allowing the Israelites to cross safely, and the Egyptian armies were drowned. In Exodus 15 the people sang praises to God for delivering them.

Here in Revelation 15, God's people sing an even greater song of praise to God for saving them from their sin and guilt, their troubles and difficulties, and bringing them safely to heaven.

On witnessing this great multitude singing praises to God, John must have felt as if he had never been to a service of worship before. I was recently in a congregation of nearly three thousand people singing some of the great hymns of praise. I was filled with a sense of awe and wonder as the congregation sang hymns such as 'Great God of wonders' and 'Mighty Christ'. It is impossible to imagine singing hymns of praise as part of a multitude which no one can number in the presence of the one who actually died on the cross to forgive me of all my sins!

The people of God are praising him not only for saving them but because his judgements are righteous. People ask why God doesn't stop wickedness and bring evil men to justice. Why doesn't he send thunderbolts down from heaven? In Romans 1:24, 26, 28 it is clear that God is not passive while sin rampages. If you trample on his law he will give you over to your sin, remove from your life all his restraining influences, and damn you eternally. In not bringing judgement on people straight away, God is patiently and graciously giving them time and opportunities to repent; but every time they reject this opportunity they are heaping more and more judgement on themselves. God is fair, righteous and just. One day evil, sin and wrongdoing will be dealt with by this God. It will all come to his judgement seat. Everything and everyone will be brought to justice and when that finally happens, the church of Jesus Christ will rejoice.

The multitude are safe and at peace for all eternity. They are gathered by the sea of crystal. The sea is a sea of glass. If the sea today looked as if it was made of glass it would be completely still and calm. The picture here is of God's people completely untroubled.

However, this sea is mixed with fire (15:2). This aspect symbolizes God's righteousness poured out in judgements on the wicked. On the day of judgement, while those who trust in Jesus Christ will know perfect peace, those outside of Christ will know the everlasting fires of God's judgement.

Even before God pours out his final judgement and before we get to heaven, as Christians we are victorious and secure. We will see in this chapter that before the final judgement God pours out judgements on this world every day; but they cannot harm God's people. The hymn-writer Augustus Toplady says that the saints in heaven are 'more happy but not more secure'. Jesus Christ has overcome the world. Even when we are caught in the middle of the storms of life, Jesus can calm the storm. A story is told of a Christian who was in one of the Twin Towers the day it was hit by the terrorists. A witness said that the people were consumed with fear and panic as they tried to escape for their lives. But in the middle of all the commotion, this Christian man calmly walked down the stairs. Knowing he was about to die, he was saying to himself, 'The Lord is my shepherd; I shall not want. He leadeth me beside the still waters… Yea, though I walk through the valley of the shadow of death, I will fear no evil: for thou art with me…' (Psalm 23, AV). Even in the worst situations, the Christian has God, and at these times he draws especially near. The hymn-writer James Grindlay Small says,

> I've found a friend, O such a Friend!
> So kind and true and tender!
> So wise a Counsellor and Guide,
> So mighty a Defender!
> From Him who loves me now so well
> What power my soul can sever?
> Shall life or death, or earth or hell?
> No! I am His for ever.

THE HEAVENLY TEMPLE (15:5-8)

After John saw the sea of crystal, he saw the heavenly temple. It is called the tabernacle of the testimony (15:5). The tabernacle was a tent, the place that God's people in the Old Testament would meet with him. In the tabernacle was the ark which contained the law of God. This law is perfect and testifies against sin. This heavenly temple of God is holy and sinless and pure: nothing that soils can ever enter in.

From this temple John sees seven angels emerge carrying seven bowls (15:6-7). They were dressed in clean shining linen and wore golden sashes around their chests (15:6). This is to show their purity and holiness. The seven angels were given seven bowls full of the wrath of God which they were to pour out (15:7).

The temple was filled with smoke from the glory of God and from his power, and no one could enter the temple until the bowls of wrath had been poured out (15:8).

The scene is suffocating in its majesty and power; a person cannot breathe in it. It is impossible for a mere creature to stand in the presence of a holy God.

These verses describe the time when the hour of judgement has come. This judgement is certain and no one will be able to reverse it. A time will come when, as Kistemaker puts it: 'God's mercy is forgotten, his compassion withheld and his patience suspended' (*Revelation*, p.433). There will be no more intercession and people's prayers for forgiveness will no longer be heard. What a terrifying day!

There was an article in *The Times* (18 October 2010) about the thirty-three Chilean miners who spent sixty-nine days afraid beneath the Chilean desert, certain they were going to die. With them was a Christian minister who read the Bible to them and prayed with them every day. The men prayed and believe God heard their prayers as all thirty-three of the men were saved. The title of the article was 'When a man screams to God then he will answer their prayer.' However, the verses here describe the time when the day of salvation and grace will be over, when a man can scream and shout and beg and plead and do whatever he wants, but God will not hear his prayer. Mercy is over, judgement has come.

The worst thing about it for everyone who suffers this eternal judgement is that they could have escaped this terrible end. We will not see this fully until the end of the book but the Lamb, Jesus Christ, is really the temple; and today he invites everyone to come to him. But one day Jesus Christ will return to this earth to judge everybody who has ever lived. On that day it will be too late to turn to him. Everyone who has rejected him as Saviour and Lord will hear the terrifying words from his lips, 'Depart from me'. But today those lips still say, 'Come to me.' He will still receive whoever comes to him.

The one who hung on that cross to save sinners is the same one who will one day send all those who rejected him to hell. One of the Puritans, Thomas Boston, said, 'To be damned by him who came to save sinners is to be doubly damned.' What an awesome, chilling thought! Today there is still access to the temple to intercede but with every day that passes we are beginning to suffocate more and more. Pray, call out to him; 'scream' to him, while you can still breathe.

SEVEN BOWLS OF WRATH (REVELATION 16)

One of the questions that people often ask is: 'Are evil people and the godless going to get away with it?'

The answer to that is 'no'. Revelation 16 shows that one day God will bring to justice those who have rebelled against him. God is slow to anger and he loves mercy. Judgement is his 'strange work' (Isaiah 28:21, AV). God holds out his arms to sinners all the day long (Isaiah 65:2). He would rather bring you to heaven than send you to hell. He will welcome the vilest sinner with open arms.

How can we be sure of that, you might ask? Because in Luke 15 Jesus tells a parable about the 'prodigal son'. Jesus told this parable in response to the accusations of some people that 'he eats with sinners'. In the story the son breaks his father's heart by more or less saying, 'I can't wait for you to die, I want my inheritance now.' He leaves home and goes to a far away country where he blows his father's money on all kinds of sinful pursuits, including prostitutes. When he doesn't have a penny left he ends up in a job looking after pigs and eating their leftovers. However, he comes to himself and decides to return to his father to see if he would take him back as one of his servants. But when he is still a long way from home, his father — who has been looking out for him — sees him and runs out to meet him. He falls on his neck and kisses him. He tells his servants to get him the best robe and puts a ring on his finger. The fatted calf, the one they kept for a special occasion, is killed. A party is held to celebrate the return of the son.

In the parable, the son represents sinners and the father represents God. In response to the self-righteous comment that this man eats with sinners, Jesus says in effect, 'Eat with sinners! You don't know the half! My father and I not only receive sinners, we run after sinners!' What a God! What a Saviour!

The world views the fact that evil people are not struck down with a thunderbolt as slackness, but God is waiting, longing for people to repent. However, in chapter 16 we are shown that God's patience towards people does not last for ever. One day his patience towards every sinner will run out.

The judgement is unrestricted. The seals affected a quarter of the earth. The trumpets affected a third; but there is no fraction with the bowls.

It is important to realize that these judgements are ordained and sanctioned personally by God (16:1). Our sins and iniquities offend the very person of God.

These judgements are also just (16:5). Society has no problem with sin, certainly not all sin; but God does; his character is at stake. The judgement of God is a just reward for sin.

Even the altar confirms the justice of these judgements (16:7). The altar is a place of mercy. It was the place where the priests in the Old Testament would go to offer sacrifices for the sins of the people. These sacrifices were made until Jesus came and 'offered one sacrifice for sins for all time' (Hebrews 10:12, NASB). Golgotha was the altar where the Lamb of God was slain for the sins of all those who would trust in him. All the wrath and judgement that should have been poured out on sinners was instead poured out on God's beloved Son. If the altar, the place of incredible mercy, where God graciously met with sinners, says God's judgements are just, then there is no way God can ever be accused of being unjust.

The objects of these judgements are the unrepentant, those who refuse this grace of God (16:9, 11).

At the beginning of chapter 16 John hears the voice of Almighty God commanding the angels to empty the bowls of wrath on the wicked. It was a loud voice (16:1) because God is full of anger against those who reject and oppose him. These judgements are poured out on the wicked every day, every week, every month, every year.

When people refuse to listen to the warning trumpets God does not allow such hardness of heart and impenitence to go unpunished until the final judgement day. When the trumpets are sounded they offer those who hear them the opportunity to repent; but when people don't repent, the bowls of wrath are poured out on them and there is no more opportunity to repent. According to Hendriksen: 'When the wicked, often warned by the trumpets of judgement, continue to harden their hearts, death finally plunges them into the hands of an angry God' (*More Than Conquerors*, p.157).

The even more worrying thing is that some cross the line between God's patience and his wrath before they die (Exodus 10:7; Matthew 12:32; Romans 1:24; 1 John 5:16). We cannot play around with God or presume upon his grace. He can warn and warn and warn us, but one day he will withdraw his Spirit from us and our hearts become hardened towards him and all we will be able to do is face judgement and eternal damnation. A time will come when he will say, 'Enough is enough.' Every day God pours out his wrath upon the unrepentant (Revelation 9:21; 16:9).

God uses every part of his universe to punish the wicked and unbelieving world. Whoever refuses to heed the warnings of the trumpets is destroyed by the bowls of wrath. A disaster or affliction could be a warning trumpet to some, but to others a bowl of wrath. These judgements take place all the time but just before the end they will be like nothing we've ever seen before. After that time will come the day of final judgement.

First four bowls (16:2-9)

The first bowl of wrath poured out malignant sores (16:2). The second bowl was poured into the sea (16:3), turning it to blood. The third bowl was poured into rivers and streams, turning them into blood, making the water undrinkable (16:4-6). The fourth bowl was poured out on the sun, causing it to scorch people with torrid temperatures (16:8-9). The first four bowls are poured out on nature.

Fifth bowl (16:10-11)

The fifth angel poured out his bowl on the throne of the beast (16:10). The throne of the beast is the centre of antichristian government. All the governments and kingdoms of this world are in God's hand. Kingdoms rise and fall at his command. This is clearly illustrated in the book of Daniel. In the first four chapters Nebuchadnezzar is a world-conquering king. But he became arrogant and God made him eat grass in a field. God used this humbling experience as a trumpet of warning, which he heeded (Daniel 4:34-37). By contrast, in Daniel chapter 5 there is another king on the throne, named Belshazzar. During a party in his palace where all kinds of debauchery and profanity take place, Belshazzar sees the fingers of a man's hand writing on a wall that he has been found wanting by God and that his kingdom is going to be divided. By the next morning Belshazzar was a corpse on the floor of his palace and his kingdom had been conquered and divided amongst the Medes and the Persians. What is recorded in the book of Daniel has happened throughout history. Kings, countries and world leaders are raised up and are struck down by the God of heaven; but instead of realizing how dependent we are in the hands of the master of the universe, we blaspheme his name and refuse to repent (16:11).

World leaders and the kings and queens of the earth are full of their own importance and power. Seldom do any of them acknowledge God. As they rule their countries and pass laws and make their plans and policies, almost never do they consider God. They seem to think that their power is in their own hands. However, an individual's, and even a country's, power is short-lived. At the time Revelation was written, Rome was the world super-power. There were many empires before Rome, and since Rome other world empires have come and gone. Lawrence James has written a brilliant book about *The Rise and Fall of the British Empire*. At the moment, America seems the world's dominant power, with the biggest economy; but one day it won't be. Apparently China has climbed to number two, whereas twenty-five years ago Japan seemed all set to be the pre-eminent economic power; now it is an 'ageing, paralysed society, apparently incapable of desperately needed reform' (*The Week*, 21 August 2010). Kingdoms rise and fall at God's command! God will not be mocked (Galatians 6:7)!

The sixth bowl (16:12-16)

The sixth bowl produces Armageddon (16:12-16). The expression Armageddon occurs only here in the entire Bible, which means it is difficult to present a convincing explanation of what Armageddon actually is. Numerous solutions have been offered; but at best these interpretations are guesses.

It is enough to say that here it describes the scene of the battle between the world under the leadership of Satan, with the help of the beast and the false prophet, and the church.

It is not a physical war but a spiritual one. It has been waged by the devil since the time of Adam and Eve; but the closer the devil comes to the end the more fiercely he plunges into battle; a battle which will include a particularly difficult time for the church. This is referred to as Satan's 'little season' and will take place just before the ultimate conflict at the end. This sixth bowl describes that 'little season' just before the final day of judgement.

In these verses several geographical places are mentioned; but as is our general rule, these are to be taken figuratively.

First, John sees the great River Euphrates dried up (16:12). This was to allow easy access for the kings of the east to get to Armageddon. The kings of the east join forces with the world against the church. This means that the road is prepared so that all antichristian powers can attack the church. It will be a time when God's law will cease to influence society. Today it is much easier to get to other parts of the world than it once was, because of air travel. Countries make joint treaties and unite together. All too often the laws they pass and the stance they take is anti-God. These things surely point to the end.

After the River Euphrates is dried up, three evil spirits come out of the mouth of the dragon, out of the mouth of the beast and out of the mouth of the false prophet (16:13). These evil spirits looked like frogs — slippery, repulsive and unclean. The lies and deceit of the dragon, the beast and the false prophet will mislead almost everyone. If it were possible, even God's elect would be deceived (Matthew 24:24). But to the elect, the ones who are sealed, these lies and deceit are abhorrent.

God's people are told to stay awake and keep their clothes on (16:15), which means that they are to be on their guard and clothe themselves in God's Word. They are to be vigilant and steadfast in the Word of God. The only way to stand at this almost impossible time is by reading the Bible and meditating upon it, obeying it, trusting its promises and hiding it in our hearts.

But when the battle is at its most ferocious, when the church seems dead and buried, when there are only a few left standing, the Lord Jesus Christ will come like a thief (16:15).

The seventh bowl (16:17-21)

The seventh bowl pours out the final judgement (16:17-21). This is when the final curtain of world history will come down. The last word belongs to God. All his enemies will be defeated and thrown into the fires of hell. They will curse God because it will be so terrible (16:20). The only people who will be saved from this awful, eternal wrath will be those trusting in the Lord Jesus Christ. As Toplady put it:

> The terrors of law and of God
>   with me can have nothing to do;
> My Saviour's obedience and blood
>   hide all my transgressions from view.

This time of judgement is unexpected (16:15). No one knows when this day will be. Make sure you are ready! It would be an awful thing to wake up in the fires of hell only to realize you will be there for ever. It is a place of outer darkness; a place where people gnash their teeth in pain and torment; a place where your conscience will trouble you for ever; a place you can never get out of.

In *The Times* (29 July 2008) there was a report on a twenty-year-old British woman, Samantha Orabator, held in Phanathong prison in Laos. Inmates described conditions in the prison as squalid. Kay Danes, an Australian who spent ten months at the prison, described the abuse and neglect at the jail. 'I've heard all the prisoners yelling at the top of their lungs, shouting for guards when one of the inmates was dying and nobody comes. Nobody ever comes.'

The Bible describes a place far worse than Phanathong prison where people scream at the top of their lungs but nobody comes. Nobody ever comes!

Deep down you believe in hell. We all think it is right when criminals get sent to prison. No one should get away with it. How much more should a holy God punish those who have sinned against him and spurned his grace and mercy? Run to the only one who can save you from such a terrible place!

SECTION 6

The fall of Babylon

(Revelation 17 - 19)

14

THE GREAT PROSTITUTE BABYLON

Revelation 17

Revelation 17 begins the sixth section of Revelation. This section comprises chapters 17 - 19.

In order to help us understand this section it may be worth reminding ourselves that five enemies of Christ have been revealed in the book of Revelation:

1. The dragon — Satan, the one behind it all!
2. The beast of the sea — persecution embodied in all the nations and governments of the world throughout history;
3. The beast of the earth — false religion and philosophy;
4. The prostitute Babylon — godless society;
5. The people who bear the mark of the beast — everyone who has not, does not or will not trust in Jesus Christ.

In the fifth section of the book, chapters 15 and 16, we saw in graphic images what will happen to the people who bear the mark of the beast, those who refuse to trust in Jesus Christ. Bowls of wrath are poured out upon them.

In the seventh and final section of the book of Revelation, the dragon's defeat will be described (chapter 20).

The sixth section of the book (chapters 17 - 19) is taken up with the prostitute Babylon, the beast of the sea and the beast of the earth. In Revelation 17:3 John is carried to the wilderness by one of the angels who poured out the seven bowls in chapters 15 and 16. In the wilderness John sees a woman who is a prostitute sitting on a scarlet beast.

THE BEAST (REVELATION 17:3)

The scarlet beast is the beast of the sea from chapter 13, which symbolizes the world as the centre of persecution. This persecution expresses itself through the governments and peoples of the world, particularly in the great world empires that follow one another in history.

In chapter 17 the beast was covered with blasphemous names and had seven heads and ten horns (17:3).

Blasphemous names (17:3)

The beast was covered in blasphemous names. These names ridicule God, his people, his church and his Word. Today, the vast majority of people are indifferent to God. Some hate him while others make fun of him. They laugh and mock those who trust him. Most people take his name in vain without even realizing it.

We hate it when people forget our name or mis-spell it or mis-pronounce it, or worse still make fun of it. Yet the vast majority of people misuse God's name every day, forget about him or even make fun of him. This is shown here by the blasphemous names that covered the beast.

Seven heads (17:3)

We discover in Revelation 17:9-11 that the seven heads are seven hills on which the woman sits. The seven heads are also seven kings. 'Five have fallen, one is, the other has not yet come; but when he does come, he must remain a little while. The beast who once was, and now is not, is an eighth king. He belongs to the seven and is going to his destruction' (17:10-11, NIV).

What does all this mean? It is like a riddle and there is no doubt that these verses are very difficult to interpret. That is why in verse 9 the angel says, 'This calls for a mind with wisdom.'

It seems most likely that the seven heads have a twofold symbolic meaning. On the one hand they refer to the embodiment of the beast at the time the book of Revelation was first written; the time of the great Roman Empire. The seven heads symbolize the seven hills that Rome was built upon. It is the great city which rules over the kings and the mighty ones of the earth. In John's day Rome was the centre of antichristian persecution, seduction, allurement and enticement; the prostitute sits on these seven hills.

But these seven heads also symbolize seven kingdoms. The five that have fallen are in all probability Ancient Babylon, Assyria, New Babylonia, Medo-Persia and Greco-Macedonia. The one that is, is Rome. The seventh is yet to come but when it comes it will have to remain some little while. This kingdom is a collective name for all antichristian government that will follow the Roman Empire. 'A little while' is a reference to the entire gospel age from Jesus' ascension to his second coming.

There is also an eighth king. He belongs to the seven and will go to his destruction. The eighth and final king will be the most terrible. This is a reference to the dominion of the Antichrist towards the close of history, or the man of sin (*cf.* 2 Thessalonians 2:3ff). The characteristic of this individual is that he opposes and exalts himself against every so-called god or object of worship. He claims to be God. He is not Satan, but Satan is behind his coming.

Even though there will be an individual Antichrist at the end, the antichristian attitude exists today. Basically, it is a denial that Jesus Christ is God, and that he became a man and came into this world to save us (1 John 2:18, 22).

The fact that the Antichrist belongs to the seven may suggest that one of the former antichristian empires will be re-established. But even though he will be terrible, he too will be destroyed.

Ten horns (17:3)

In Revelation 17:12-14 we see that the ten horns are ten kings who have not yet received a kingdom, but who for one hour will receive authority as kings along with the beast. 'They have one purpose and will give their power and authority to the beast. They will make war against the Lamb, but the Lamb will overcome them because he is Lord of lords and King of kings — and with him will be his called, chosen and faithful followers' (17:13-14, NIV).

As we said earlier, the number 10 is symbolic of completeness. This refers to all the kings and mighty ones of this world throughout history. They reign for just one hour; which means that all the great men and emperors of this world will come and go. Even the longest, most impressive reigns are short in the light of the whole of time, never mind eternity.

They all have another thing in common: they help the beast in his conflict with the Lamb. They all have a hatred of God (Revelation 17:13-14). This will be especially true just before the end of time, when all the kingdoms of the world at that time will lend their power to assist the Antichrist. However, it is true to some degree of the kingdoms of the world throughout time. Once God's Word says that what a country is doing is wrong and they should repent, those rulers and governments turn their back on God. When the church stands up against antichristian ideas or refuses to obey antichristian laws, then in some parts of the world it is persecuted and in others marginalized and written off as old-fashioned or extreme.

Even though all of these kingdoms appear awesome, in the end the Lamb will conquer.

Once was, now is not, and will come up out of the abyss (17:8)

Kingdoms come and go, but behind them all is the beast.

First the beast was. This refers to all the kingdoms and empires of the world that once were. In their day they were so powerful and ruled the world. They were arrogant and proud and oppressed their enemies — the Babylonian empire, the Medo-Persian empire, the Greek empire and so on. But all of these kingdoms that 'once were', in which the beast had been embodied, perished. Each one of them 'once was but now is not'.

However, the astonishing thing is that the beast will come up out of the abyss again in a different form. When one world empire falls another one rises. Again and again the beast appears in a different form and will do right up until the final judgement day.

There will never be a time when evil will not trouble the church; the form changes, but the essence remains throughout history. Evil keeps re-inventing itself. For example, in this hi-tech age the internet has allowed people to look at pornography in a way they could not have dreamt of years ago.

All whose names are not in the book of life (that is, who do not trust in Jesus Christ) are astonished when they see the beast (17:8). They are in awe of him and follow him.

The main reason why people will not trust in Jesus Christ is because they refuse to have him rule over them. They do not want him as Lord of their lives. No one likes being restricted and answerable and told what to do. Everyone wants to do things their own way. Frank Sinatra famously sang a song called 'My way'. The song includes lyrics like: 'I've lived a life that's full, I travelled each and every highway, and more, much more than this, I did it my way.' It goes on to say, 'I planned each charted course, each careful step along the byway, and more, much more than this, I did it my way.' It finishes by saying, 'The record shows I took the blows and did it my way.' These words sum up what every person with no thought for God thinks about their own lives. However, at the end of the person's life, chillingly the beast will whisper, 'Actually, you did it my way!'

THE WOMAN (REVELATION 17:4-7)

On the beast sits a woman. She is dressed in purple and scarlet and is glittering with gold, precious stones and pearls. She has a golden cup in her hand, filled with abominable things and the filth of her adulteries (17:4). The image is of a woman who is glamorous but not beautiful. If she walked down the street she would turn heads because she looks so provocative; but behind it all, and on closer inspection, there is no real beauty. The golden cup is so enticing and promises every pleasure imaginable, but inside it is filthy.

The prostitute Babylon represents godless society. She is the notorious prostitute with whom the kings of the earth have committed adultery and whose adulteries have intoxicated the inhabitants of the earth (17:1-2).

Prostitutes try to lure men into having sex with them. Similarly, this prostitute tries to entice people away from God into all kinds of immorality and idolatry (17:4-5). An idol is the thing, or things, that are the most important in a person's life, and which take the place of God. The prostitute makes people think these idols are better, more worthy and satisfying than God. Idols can be things which in and of themselves are fine, but can take over your life and become too important — jobs, social life, possessions, hobbies and so on.

The world seems so wonderful and the things on offer seem so tempting. There are all kinds of immoralities on offer to young people today — drink, drugs, sex, pornography, gambling and so much more in our pleasure-mad society. It all seems so exciting and pleasurable. Adverts on television and in magazines and newspapers show you things you think you just have to have even if it means having huge credit card debts to obtain them.

The golden cup that the great prostitute offers to you promises to satisfy all your wants and needs, but it leaves you feeling dirty and will eventually lead you to destruction. It never satisfies. You will always want more.

This prostitute at the time Revelation was first written was specifically Rome, which like ancient Babylon had gained a world-wide reputation for luxury, corruption and power. But not only is she Rome; she is the mother of all prostitutes so her evil vice spawns the entire world throughout the whole of time. She is pictured in 17:1 as seated on many waters, which is a reference to all the many people who are subject to her evil influence. It extends to our day and age. Western society today is marked out by the flaunting of filth and all kinds of immorality.

This great prostitute also entices people into gross and corrupting materialism. After she has fallen in Revelation 18:11-15 she mourns

161

because no one buys her goods any more. Today we are obsessed with nice things and having as much stuff we can afford (or, in most cases, things we can't afford). We live in a capitalist society that is luxury-orientated. There is evidence everywhere of gross and corrupting materialism. In sport, cricketers cheat in order to get more money. In politics, there is a scandal over MPs' expenses. Our debt record shows our obsession with luxury and pleasure.

However, the prostitute's greatest sin is that she has gorged herself on the blood of God's people. She is the one responsible for the suffering and bloodshed brought upon the struggling church. Revelation 17:6 says she is drunk with the blood of the saints. She kills those who refuse to participate in her abominable idolatries.

Christians who refuse to go along with this way of life suffer. The fact that a Christian's life is so different from this way of living, or at least should be, irritates and gets under the skin of this great prostitute. As a result, Christians are laughed at, marginalized, ignored, left out, mocked, persecuted and even killed. All who live godly lives will suffer persecution (2 Timothy 3:12).

WHY DO YOU WONDER? (17:7)

Do you ever wonder at evil? Are you ever amazed by what you read in the newspapers or watch on the television? Are there things in your own life that you've done or do and you are utterly ashamed of and afterwards can't believe you've done them? Are there people you know who have done things you are shocked by?

In Revelation 17:6 John sees things that utterly amaze him and leave him wondering greatly. But the angel wonders at why he is wondering (17:7)! The great prostitute, this world, is borne along directly by the power of hell. We should never be surprised by the extent or depths of evil. This world is fuelled by the powers of the devil and hell itself. It is only because of God's common or restraining grace that things are not worse. Only God knows what our society would be like if evil were given free rein. Rev. Alun McNabb tells about a neighbour who was an atheist. One day this neighbour was talking to Mr McNabb complaining about the state of the nation and how society seemed to be getting worse and worse. Mr McNabb said to him, 'You're getting what you wanted, a godless society!' The more a country or people turn their back on God, the more evil things become.

THE SELF-DESTRUCTIVE POWER OF EVIL
(REVELATION 17:16)

In the end evil will self-destruct; it has a self-destructive power within it. The beast will hate the prostitute and bring her to ruin. She will be left naked, her flesh eaten and she will be burnt with fire (17:16). The pleasures of sin disappoint in the end. Pubs and clubs are full of fun and excitement at the start of a Friday or Saturday night; but by the end of the night, people have fallen out, had fights, got jealous, ended up doing things that at the time seemed so much pleasure and fun but now have left them feeling guilty and wrecked their marriages, families and relationships. They wake up in the middle of the night or in the morning feeling empty, hating themselves and those they've committed shameful acts with.

People become infatuated with the pleasures of sin and harden themselves against God. But in the end they loathe themselves. The danger is that if you harden your heart towards God for too long, he will harden your heart and then it will be too late (17:17).

Don't be enticed and give your life to this world and all that it offers. Even the things that in and of themselves are not sinful cannot ultimately satisfy a person. The best the world can offer, and the biggest achievements you can possibly have, cannot fulfil your deepest needs.

Jonny Wilkinson (*The Times*, 21 November 2009) powerfully proved this point when he described what it was like winning the Rugby World Cup for England. It was the pinnacle of his career and something almost every school boy in the country dreams of. But this is what he said:

> *I had already begun to feel the elation slipping away from me during the lap of honour around the field. I couldn't believe that all the effort was losing its worth so soon. This was something I had fantasised about achieving since I was a child. In my head I had reached the peak of the mountain and now all that was left was to slowly descend the other side. I'd just achieved my greatest ambition and it felt a bit empty.*

15

FALLEN IS BABYLON THE GREAT!

Revelation 18

INTRODUCTION

In Revelation 18:1 John sees another angel, who announces the fall of the prostitute Babylon, coming down from heaven. The angel has great authority and with a strong voice he cries: 'Fallen, fallen is Babylon the great!' (ESV). The fall of Babylon is so sure that it is announced as though it has already taken place.

As was pointed out in the last chapter, the prostitute Babylon has a twofold symbolism. On one level it represents the Rome of John's day, which was the centre of power, luxury and fierce persecution and antagonism towards the Christian faith. But on another level this prostitute is symbolic of all godless countries, societies and peoples of all time, including our own.

Chapter 18 records a dirge over the cursed city. The dirge is in three parts.

Firstly (18:1-8), an angel with great authority announces that Babylon the great is fallen while another angel calls God's people out of the city and proclaims judgement against her many crimes and sins.

Secondly (18:9-20), we hear the mournful lament of three groups in society that have profited from the great city's unquenchable appetite for material abundance. These are the kings of the world who had committed adultery with her (18:9-10), the merchants who supplied her with anything and everything she wanted (18:11-17a) and the maritime industry that brought her cargo from around the world (18:17b-20).

Thirdly, there is the actual fall of the great city (18:21-24). The entire dirge is poetic in language and form.

THE ANNOUNCEMENT (18:1-8)

The announcement of Babylon's desolation comes in two sections.

In verses 1-3 an angel whose very presence illumines the earth comes down from heaven. This angel reflects the radiance and glory of God. With great authority this angel announces that Babylon has fallen. All that this once great city has to look forward to is death, mourning, famine and complete ruin. She is now a home for demons, evil spirits and unclean and detestable birds. Babylon the great is now like a dreadful prison. According to Mounce: 'It is a prophetic picture of absolute desolation where the proud achievements of the human race become the demonic haunts of unclean and detestable creatures' (*Revelation*, p.326). It may seem that God has forgotten Babylon's sins; but on the day that Babylon falls it will be clear that he has most certainly not!

Then, in verses 4-8, another voice from heaven calls the people of God to come out of the city, for it is about to receive a double portion of the suffering it inflicted on others. This call to leave Babylon is addressed to God's people in all ages. Babylon represents godless society throughout the whole of time and those who trust in Jesus Christ are called to come out from among her and be separate (2 Corinthians 6:17). A true Christian will find it impossible to carry on wilfully sinning. Christ and sin cannot live at peace in the same heart. There will be certain things that a Christian cannot do and certain places a Christian cannot go.

This does not mean that they should have nothing to do with non-Christians and lock themselves away from the world. Christians should be friendly, loving, winsome and as sociable as they can, but not be ensnared and enticed by Babylon's sins. Those who set their heart on Babylon and all that it offers will perish with her.

The torment and mourning she endures will be the exact equivalent of her pride and arrogance (18:7). She will be paid back in judgement exactly what her sins deserve. People who sin against God will be judged according to what they have done. Every person will get their just deserts.

THE LAMENT (18:9-20)

Every department of her existence is destroyed and all her inhabitants weep greatly.

The kings and mighty men, the men of influence (18:9-10)

The kings and mighty men, the men of influence will weep and mourn over her (18:9-10). They yielded to her temptations and have enjoyed her luxuries. They are terrified at her torment and are amazed at the fact that judgement could fall so suddenly: 'For in one hour your judgement has come' (18:10, NKJV).

There are many successful, powerful, rich, famous and influential people in the world today. They are full of their own importance and consumed with their own success and wealth. They enjoy the power they have and the lavish lifestyles they lead. But one day these people, along with all people outside of Jesus Christ, will be terrified because this world they've lived for and whose pleasures they've indulged in, will come to an end. This will happen suddenly. Before they can do anything about it, torment will be upon them.

The merchants (18:11-17)

The merchants also mourn over this one-time great city because no one buys their produce any more (18:11-17). In these verses various materials that are used to make articles of luxury are listed. Various kinds of costly garments are mentioned: fine linen, purple, silk and scarlet. The best in the line of food and drink: wine, oil, fine flour, wheat. All are destroyed. The apostle's picture is based on conditions that prevailed at the time he wrote, but the picture of Babylon is true of every age. The food and drink we enjoy, the nice clothes we wear, our hi-tech gadgets, our houses and cars; one day all will be destroyed. None of them will last for ever.

So many people set their hearts on the goods and luxuries of the world without any thought for the next world. This is perfectly illustrated in the story of the rich fool in Luke 12:16-21. He was a farmer who had a bumper harvest which made him a very rich man. He had no thought for God or anyone else but instead simply ate, drank and enjoyed himself. But one night God said to him, 'You fool, this very night your soul is required of you' (Luke 12:20, NASB). When a person stands before God, his wealth and riches are of no use. 'What will it profit a man if he gains the whole world and loses his own soul? Or what will a man give in exchange for his soul?' (Mark 8:36-37, NKJV).

Seafaring men (18:18-20)

The last group who mourn for her are the seafaring men (18:18-20). These comprise the captains, the passengers intent on business, the sailors, and as many as gain their living by the sea (e.g. exporters, importers and fishermen). They see from afar the smoke of Babylon's flames. They recall her former greatness and splendour and they can hardly believe their eyes when they see her total ruin. They are so devastated that they throw dust on their heads and cry out and weep (18:19).

BABYLON'S ACTUAL FALL (18:21-24)

A strong angel picks up a great millstone and hurls it into the sea, saying that with such violence the great city Babylon will be thrown down, never to be found again.

In verses 21-24 the phrase 'no more at all' occurs six times. The city in general will be thrown down, never to be found again (18:21); the sound of music will never be heard again (18:22); no workmen of any trade will ever be found again (18:22); the sound of the millstone will never be heard again (18:22); light will never shine again (18:23); there will be no more love, 'the voice of bridegroom and bride will never be heard in you again' (18:23, NIV). Imagine it! No love, absolute darkness, none of our basic needs met, no music!

It is impossible to imagine how awful it will be; never being able to hear music ever again; never tasting good food ever again; never having your thirst quenched; absolute darkness; horrible loneliness; never feeling loved or cared for. What a terrible plight to find yourself in for all eternity!

The gold and glamour of the great prostitute Babylon has deceived the wicked. She has caused them to wander farther and farther from God. But now she is ruined. She has gone up in flames and all those who have been enticed by her share in her torment. No wonder the Bible urges us to flee from the wrath to come!

According to Hendriksen:

> *The pleasure mad, arrogant world, with all its seductive luxuries and pleasures, with its antichristian philosophy and culture, with its teeming multitudes that have forsaken God and have lived according to the lusts of the flesh and the desires of the mind, shall perish. The wicked suffer eternal despair. This doom will not be complete until the day of final judgement*
>
> (*More Than Conquerors*, p.178).

16

THE MARRIAGE SUPPER OF THE LAMB

Revelation 19:1-10

In chapter 18 John sees the fall of Babylon, which symbolizes the fall of this godless world. The fall is devastating. The inhabitants of Babylon weep and cry out when they see the smoke of her burning. The place that was once home to the proud achievements of the human race has become the demonic haunt of unclean and detestable creatures. Her fall is final. She is thrown down never to rise again. All the things that people once enjoyed are gone for ever. No more music, no more light, no more love!

HALLELUJAH! (REVELATION 19:1-5)

But at the beginning of chapter 19 John's attention is turned from this scene of absolute devastation to one of total victory. The cameras move from earth to heaven. John hears something like the roar of a great multitude in heaven. He uses the words 'something like' because what he hears is indescribable. The nearest we can imagine is the roar that you hear at a major sporting event or at the celebrations that occur after a team has been victorious. According to Barnes (*The Meaning of Sport*, p.111), after England won the

Rugby World Cup in 2003 there were three-quarters of a million people lining the brief route through the West End of London — ten deep at the pavements, shinning up lamp-posts, balanced on litter bins, hanging from windows, crowding onto balconies: cheering and cheering and cheering! The players had no idea how much it had meant to the cacophonous crowd and what heroes they were.

That scene in London cannot begin to compare with what John saw at the beginning of chapter 19. It is a loud thunderous noise. The people cannot contain their happiness and joy.

This great multitude is shouting 'Hallelujah!' This means 'Praise God.' The multitude is full of praise for God because they have seen the judgement of God against a sinful world that has hated God and persecuted his people. The judgement God poured out in chapter 18 on the ungodly world could have been poured out on them too; but God saved them and rescued them from the power of Satan. He has vindicated his honour and saved his people.

His judgement demonstrates his glory and power. Heaven is not embarrassed about the fierce judgement of God. The ferocity of the judgements simply shows the sinfulness and the seriousness of sin.

In the end, justice will be done. The first readers of Revelation were people who had really suffered and seen their fellow-Christians killed. Maybe they were wondering whether evil does ultimately triumph. In Revelation 19:2, John is shown that justice will be done. God has the last word.

The whole of creation rejoices: the twenty-four elders and the four living creatures fell down and worshipped God (19:4) along with everyone both great and small (19:5), men and angels. One day every knee will bow and every tongue will confess that Jesus Christ is Lord. Even those who deny him, are indifferent to him, hate him, one day will bow down to him.

During the first performance of Handel's *Messiah* in London, attended by King George II, as the first notes of the triumphant Hallelujah Chorus rang out, the king rose to his feet and remained standing until the end of the chorus. The exact reason why the king stood is lost to history; but as well as the fact that he was clearly moved by the performance, one of the most popular explanations is that (as was, and is, the custom) one stands in the presence of royalty as a sign of respect. The Hallelujah Chorus clearly places Christ as the King of kings. In standing, King George II accepted that he too was subject to the Lord of lords.

MARRIAGE SUPPER OF THE LAMB (19:6-10)

Everywhere in the Bible the love relationship between a bridegroom and his bride is compared to the love relationship between Christ and his church (Ephesians 5:32; Revelation 21:9; Song of Solomon).

In Revelation 19:6-10 the actual wedding supper is described. In order to appreciate how breathtaking the marriage supper of the Lamb will be, it is necessary to have some understanding of the marriage customs of the Hebrews.

The first stage is the betrothal. This is like our engagement, but far more binding. From this moment onwards the couple are totally committed to each other and are legally husband and wife (2 Corinthians 11:2). However, there is an interval between the betrothal and the wedding supper. During this time the groom pays the dowry to the father of the bride. As the interval between the betrothal and the wedding supper comes to an end, the bride begins to prepare and adorn herself. The groom, dressed in his best attire and accompanied by his friends, proceeds to the home of the betrothed. He receives his bride and takes her back to his home. Finally there is the wedding supper. The festivities would last seven or more days.

Now think about it in relation to our relationship with God. Before the creation of the world he chose us to be his bride. Before he put the sun, the moon and the stars in their place, and built every mountain and rolled out every sea, he set his love upon us.

Throughout the Old Testament the wedding was announced. The prophets all foretold a Saviour who was coming.

At Golgotha this Saviour paid the dowry for us. With his own blood he bought us.

At conversion we were betrothed to him. When we confessed our sins to him and asked him to forgive us and took him as our Saviour he accepted us and joined us to him.

Every day we prepare ourselves for him, longing for the day he will come to our home on this earth and take us with him to heaven. What a day it will be when we sit down at the marriage supper!

John is so overwhelmed that he falls at the angel's feet to worship him. But the angel sharply rebukes him and says, 'Don't do it … worship God' (19:10). Only God is to be worshipped.

We are not to make idols even of the very best of men because even they are men at best. Dr Martyn Lloyd-Jones was a great preacher. Many of his sermons are printed in books today and are read by people all over the world. He was the minister of Westminster Chapel in London and thousands would come to hear him preach. Mr Higham went to see him as he was dying and as he was about to leave, Dr Lloyd-Jones called him back and said, 'Just remember, my boy, I'm just a sinner saved by grace.' God alone is to be worshipped.

17

THE RIDER ON THE WHITE HORSE

Revelation 19:11-21

THE RIDER ON THE WHITE HORSE (19:11-21)

John sees heaven open for the second time. In chapter 4 a door is open for John to enter heaven; but in 19:11 the whole of heaven is open for the Lord and his armies to leave and engage in a spiritual battle against enemy forces.

The Lord Jesus is the rider on the white horse, a mighty military figure. He is going to judge with justice and make war on all his enemies.

Just

When Christ returns to this world all his enemies who have fought against him will be brought to justice.

God is just. If people break his law and sin against him, his justice demands that they are punished eternally in hell. He cannot let

175

anyone off. He cannot overlook sin. Justice has to be done or God is no longer God.

This is why the gospel is such good news, because the first time Jesus Christ came to earth he came to deal with his people's sin. He came to save them from their sin and all its consequences. God has to punish sin and on the cross Jesus Christ took the sins of his people upon himself. The Bible says he became sin for us (2 Corinthians 5:21). Instead of God's just anger being poured out on his people, it was poured out on Jesus Christ. Sin was dealt with and so God's justice was satisfied and, amazingly, whoever trusts in the work that Jesus Christ did on Golgotha can know sins forgiven and have peace with God. At the cross of Jesus Christ justice and mercy met.

However, Revelation 19:11-21 is clear that he is coming to make war against all those who do not trust in him and have rejected him. There will be no mercy.

The colour white symbolizes victory, so he will be the victorious conqueror. He will overcome all his enemies.

He is identified by two names: Faithful and True.

Faithful

He is faithful; reliable and constant. We can be moody and fickle but Jesus Christ is always the same. He is the same yesterday, today and for ever (Hebrews 13:8). He fulfils everything the Scriptures reveal about him. You can rely on everything the Bible says about him. He is faithful to everything the Bible has revealed about him.

If you confess your sins to him he will definitely forgive every one of them because he has promised to and he is faithful (1 John 1:9). He will preserve his people and present them blameless on judgement day (1 Corinthians 1:8-9; 1 Thessalonians 5:23-24). Everyone who is suffering can rest in the knowledge that he will be faithful to them (1 Peter 4:19). Even when we are unfaithful, he continues to be faithful. His faithfulness is not dependent on us (2 Timothy 2:13). He is a loyal, faithful friend, one that 'sticks closer than a brother' (Proverbs 18:24).

He will be faithful in executing justice against his enemies.

True

He is true. He is dependable and can be trusted to keep his word. Everything he says is true. He is real and not in any way false. Jesus is truth personified (John 14:6). The Christian faith is the truth (Galatians 2:5; Ephesians 1:13). Jesus came to show us the truth (John 1:17), and only by his Spirit is this truth revealed to us (John 16:13).

We live in a time when people don't know what or whom to believe. It is difficult to know whom you can and can't trust. Life seems full of broken promises. We've seen recently how the financial world cannot be relied upon. People have seen the value of their properties or their investments plummet and even their businesses fold and jobs lost. Wedding vows are broken and families split up. Maybe you've been in love but have had your heart broken or you've confided in your friend and they've betrayed your trust. Politicians rarely keep their promises. In *The Week* (23 October 2010) it was reported that before the election the Liberal Democrats promised that there would be no rise in tuition fees. It was their flagship electoral slogan and they benefitted handsomely from it. Now they are saying that the current cap of £3,290 a year on student fees should be lifted to £7,000. People who voted for them feel cheated because they've gone back on their word.

But how can we know that Jesus Christ is the truth?

One reason is that there were eyewitnesses of all the things he said and did (in particular his resurrection), and these eyewitnesses wrote it down in the Bible.

In my job I sometimes have to sort out fights between pupils. If a fight has occurred at a lunchtime I have to interview pupils to find out what happened. Everyone wants to get out of the last lesson to tell me about it! However, most of them have only heard what others have said about what happened and so they are sent back to lessons rather sharpish. But then someone comes to my office and says, 'Sir, I saw everything. I saw the punches flying in; I could hear the hair being torn; I could smell the sweat and see the blood. I saw everything, Sir; I couldn't have been closer to the action; I was ringside!'

The men who wrote their accounts about Jesus' life and death and resurrection could not have been closer to the action. They were ringside! Their conclusion was that he was the truth, the Son of God, the Saviour of the world. They were so convinced that they were prepared to die for him. Even his enemies could find no fault with him. Even one of the soldiers whose job it was to put him on the cross said, 'Surely he was the Son of God' (Matthew 27:54, NIV).

Another reason why we can be sure he is the truth is because the Bible says so. The Bible was written by over forty people over a period of 1500 years and yet there is a remarkable unity and coherence throughout the whole book. The only explanation is that this book is in fact the work of a single divine author. All its prophecies to date have been fulfilled and its message is still relevant thousands of years later. The Bible has also had a powerful influence in the lives of millions of people and has transformed communities, whole countries and even the whole of civilization.

We know Jesus Christ is true because he has stood the test of time. He is no novelty. Christianity has been subjected to persecution and ridicule since Christ came into the world; but it still survives today. Men have tried to disprove the Bible but have failed. It keeps being true.

In my job I also have to interview pupils who have done something wrong. Nearly all pupils will at first deny any wrongdoing. And so my job is to cross-examine them; to come at them from different angles. Eventually the truth comes out. The Bible has been cross-examined for thousands of years. Men have come at it from different angles but it keeps being true!

Even the Jewish historian Josephus wrote of Jesus Christ:

> About this time lived Jesus, a wise man, if indeed one ought to
> call him a man. For he was an achiever of extraordinary deeds
> ... Pilate condemned him to be crucified, those who had come
> to love him did not cease to do so; for he appeared to them on
> the third day restored to life
> (Maier, Josephus: The Essential Writings, pp.264-5).

In this uncertain, unreliable world, come to one who is true. You can trust him with all your heart. You can hand over your life to him, your future to him, your worries to him. He will not ever let you down, in life or in death.

Eyes as a flame of fire

As we observed in the opening chapter of Revelation, the white rider's eyes are as a flame of fire (19:12). He knows and sees everything and can read the hearts of us all. That the Lord Jesus Christ sees everything is both a frightening and comforting thought. It's frightening because he knows everything about us. Nothing you or I have ever done, thought or said has gone unnoticed. Every shameful secret we've hidden; every dirty thought we've had; every spiteful thing we've said; what we're like on our own. He's seen it all. When he comes back to this world everything will be revealed.

But it is also comforting because all the things he knows about us can be forgiven. There's nothing he doesn't know about you or might find out that will change his mind about you. In John 21:17 Peter says to the Lord Jesus Christ, 'Lord, you know everything.' I don't know about you but I've got some bad things in my 'everything'! But these eyes that are like flames of fire are also eyes that look on us with compassion. He knows you better than you know yourself, he knows your 'everything' and yet still says, 'Come.'

Lord of all

On his head are many crowns which proclaim his universal kingship. He is Lord of all. He is Lord of every sphere of our lives. There is nothing outside his control. Your family, teachers, lecturers, friends, colleagues, neighbours and boss; the bully in your class; the government of your country; every world leader; the rich and famous; the influential and important — he's got the whole world in his hand.

A name that no one knows except himself

He has a name written that no one knows except himself (19:12). In the book of Revelation Christ has many names: the Lamb, Faithful and True, Lord of lords and King of kings, Morning Star and others. These names reveal wonderful truths about the Lord Jesus. But in addition to these many titles he has a name which no one knows but himself. We will never be able to understand fully the mystery of God. We can only know what he reveals to us.

However, we should seek him with all our hearts and plead with him to give us a greater understanding and appreciation of who he is. We may get to know Christ better and better by attending church, taking communion, showing kindness, having a forgiving spirit, being full of love, being thankful, obeying his commands, studying the Bible, singing hymns, praying in secret every day and attending the church prayer meeting.

War!

He was clothed in a robe dipped in blood and his name was called the Word of God (19:13). His robe that was dipped in blood is a reference to Isaiah 63:4-6. It does not refer to his own blood that he shed on Golgotha but to the blood of his enemies.

In John 1:1 he is called the Word, *logos*. This is because in him God fully expresses and reveals himself. If you want to know what God is like, look at Jesus Christ.

The armies of heaven accompany him clothed in fine linen (19:14). This army includes angels and all the saints as both will accompany the Lord Jesus on his return to this world (Matthew 24:31; Mark 13:27; Luke 9:26; 1 Thessalonians 4:13-18; 2 Thessalonians 1:7-10). The saints are white and pure. They were once sinners but they have been made clean.

Out of his mouth proceeds a sharp sword with which he will strike down the nations. He will rule them with an iron rod and will pour out on his enemies the full fury of the wrath of God Almighty. On his robe and his thigh he has the name written, KING OF KINGS AND LORD OF LORDS (Revelation 19:15-16).

When he first came to this world he came humbly. He came incognito. He was born to a humble teenage Hebrew maid. He was born in an insignificant place called Bethlehem, in a stable where his mother Mary wrapped him in cloths and laid him in a trough that animals ate out of.

But when he comes next time, his second coming, he will come in great power and glory. All the angels of heaven and all his people who have already died will accompany him. A trumpet will sound and every eye will behold him. He is not coming next time with the good news of the gospel but he is coming with a sharp sword to judge the nations.

In Revelation 19:17-21 the battle that the rider on the white horse has come to wage is described. This is the final battle of Almighty God against all the forces of evil (see Revelation 16:14). It is the destruction of the beast and the false prophet (beast of the sea and beast of the earth). The outcome of the battle is never in doubt.

In verses 17 and 18 an angel with a loud voice cries out to all the birds flying in mid-air to come and gather together for the great supper of God so that they may eat the flesh of kings, generals and mighty men, of horses and their riders, and the flesh of all people, free and slave, small and great; in other words, everyone who has followed these two beasts. It is an immense slaughter. In verse 20 the beast and false prophet are thrown alive into the lake of fire.

In these verses, John sees the whole world of unbelief gathered for the final assault upon the church. The battle itself is not described. We are simply told that the antichristian forces are gathered together against Christ and his army, and that they are put to rout.

FOUR DOWN, ONE TO GO!

In Revelation 15 and 16 we saw the end of the men and women who bear the mark of the beast. In Revelation 17 and 18 we were shown the fall of Babylon. Christ's victory over the beast of the earth and the beast of the sea was described in Revelation 19:11ff. One foe remains, the leader of them all. It is the dragon, Satan!

SECTION 7

The great consummation

(Revelation 20 - 22)

18

A THOUSAND YEARS, THE BINDING OF SATAN AND A GREAT WHITE THRONE

Revelation 20

INTRODUCTION

Chapter 20 marks the beginning of the seventh and final section of the book of Revelation. It is important to remember that the seven main sections in the book of Revelation are parallel sections. The book is not in chronological order. The seven sections look at the same picture from different angles. Each section starts at the time of Christ and takes us to the very brink of the end of time. However, at the same time, as Grier says, 'The book moves with increasing crescendo to the climax' (*The Momentous Event*, p.98).

This is certainly true of the seventh section (chapters 20 - 22). It covers the whole of human history from the time the Lord Jesus came into the world right up to his second coming when he will return to this world to judge it. But this section reaches the climax of the book and deals with the great consummation, the absolute completion of everything; how it will all finish.

Revelation 20 is interpreted in three main ways. The three interpretations are known as 'premillennialism', 'postmillennialism' and 'amillennialism'. The three interpretations differ over the meaning of the thousand years (20:2-3).

It seems to me that the interpretation that fits in with the rest of the teaching of the Bible is amillennialism. This approach sees the thousand years as being symbolic of world history between Christ's first and second coming. Just before Christ's second coming there will be widespread apostasy, that is, a turning away from the Lord Jesus Christ and opposition to the gospel, which will reach its climax in the appearance of the Antichrist. The Lord Jesus Christ will suddenly return to this world and conquer Satan and the forces of evil and will judge all people. On this day, the dead will be resurrected and they too will be judged.

THE BINDING OF SATAN (REVELATION 20:1-3)

In the opening verse of Revelation 20 John sees an angel coming down out of heaven. The angel has a great chain in his hand and a key. He overpowers the dragon, who is the devil or Satan, and binds him for a thousand years. He throws him into the abyss and locks it. He does this to keep Satan from deceiving the nations any more until the thousand years are ended. After the thousand years, Satan will be set free for a short time.

What does it all mean? As we have seen, Revelation is a book full of symbols. We are not to take these symbols literally but try to find out what they mean. This is true of Revelation 20 as well.

Revelation 19:19ff took us to the very end of history, to judgement day. Revelation 20 takes us back to the time when the Lord Jesus Christ came into this world, died on the cross and rose again. This is the beginning of what we call the new dispensation.

In the old dispensation — before Christ came — all nations except the Jews were in the clutches of Satan. Acts 14:6 says that in past generations God allowed all the nations to walk in their own ways. Only the Jews really knew about the one true and living God. Even though it is the case today that the devil has 'blinded the minds of unbelievers' (2 Corinthians 4:4, NIV), it was even more true during the old dispensation. In those days it seemed as if the gospel would never advance throughout the world but would be confined to a little nation east of the Mediterranean.

However, there were prophecies which foretold that this condition would change. Psalm 2:8 (NKJV) says, 'I will give you the nations for your inheritance and the uttermost parts of the earth for your possession.' Psalm 72:8 (NKJV) says, 'He shall have dominion also from sea to sea, and from the River to the ends of the earth.' These prophecies talk of a time when God's kingdom would advance and spread from sea to sea and to the uttermost parts of the earth. But in order for the Lord Jesus Christ to establish his kingdom throughout the world, Satan must first be mastered and bound.

The prophecies were fulfilled when the Lord Jesus Christ came into this world and are symbolized in this chapter by Satan being bound.

Temptation

The work of binding Satan started when the Lord Jesus Christ was tempted by him in the wilderness (Matthew 4:1-11).

At the very beginning of time God made man and woman, Adam and Eve. They were perfect and he placed them in a garden called Eden. It was paradise. They could eat of any fruit in the garden except one. If they ate from the tree of the knowledge of good and evil, they would die (Genesis 2:17). However, the devil, Satan, came to Eve in the form of a serpent and tempted her into eating the forbidden fruit; and she in turn gave some to Adam. Thus Adam and Eve gave in to the devil and disobeyed God, and sin and death entered the world. The fall did not only affect Adam and Eve, but also the entire human race. Because Adam was our representative, sin is part of every person's nature. The consequences are enormous. We are under the power and influence of the devil.

Jesus Christ came to save us from the dominion of Satan. To do this, he would need to succeed where Adam and Eve failed. He would have to overcome all the devil would throw at him. Matthew 4:1-11 records how the devil tempted the Lord Jesus Christ in the wilderness for forty days and forty nights. There were three temptations in particular. Each time Jesus resisted the temptation and overcame the devil. Thus, Satan became less powerful and the binding of Satan began.

Missionary work

This is seen more clearly when Jesus sent out seventy of his disciples (Luke 10:1-12). He sent them out to proclaim the gospel, the good news about Jesus Christ. When they came back they said to him, 'Lord, even the demons are subject to us in your name' (Luke 10:17, NKJV). In the next verse Jesus explains why. He says, 'I beheld Satan fall from heaven.' For the gospel to spread and advance throughout the world, Satan needs to be bound.

Christ's death and resurrection

But the ultimate victory came when the Lord Jesus Christ died on the cross and rose again. It was then that Satan was defeated and bound for a thousand years. Christ's death and resurrection signalled the binding of Satan and he cannot prevent the spread of the gospel throughout the earth.

Thousand years

As has already been said, the thousand years is symbolic of the time from Christ's first coming right up until a very short time before his second coming. During this time Satan is bound, which means the gospel will advance and people from every nation will be saved. Churches will be established and Christianity will spread. Satan's influence on earth is curtailed. He cannot prevent the church extending throughout the world. Through the preaching of God's Word, the Bible, and the work of the Holy Spirit, people are brought from darkness to light. This means that whereas they were in the dark about God, their sin, and heaven and hell, they have now been brought into the glorious light of the gospel. They see their sin but also see that there is a Saviour, Jesus Christ, who can forgive and save to the uttermost all who come to him.

Whereas once the church consisted of the Jews and was restricted to a country in the Middle East, now the church is universal, international. The gospel is spreading to the four corners of the earth. Moreover, history records how over the last two thousand years or so Christianity has exerted tremendous influence for good upon the whole world and human life.

Not bound in every sense

However, Satan is not bound in every sense. The binding of Satan does not eliminate wickedness from the earth or render Satan immobile. Even though he has been defeated he will not be cast into hell until the very end of time. He is chained; but like a wild animal on a chain he doesn't sit still. He will move around and rage as far as his chain will allow him to go. He is determined to cause as much havoc as possible. He tempts Christians, tries to make them doubt God and their own salvation, creates splits in churches and causes Christians to fall out. He persecutes them and reminds them of all the sins they've committed.

But as evil rages and the devil tries to cause as much havoc as possible, we need to remember that he's chained, even though it doesn't seem like it at times. This is illustrated in *Pilgrim's Progress*. Christian was afraid when he saw two lions on his way to the Promised Land. Bunyan says, 'the lions were chained' and then adds, 'but he saw not the chains'. That is true today. At times the devil can torment and trouble us and get us down; but we need to remember that he's chained!

His power is limited and one thing he cannot do during the thousand-year period is to prevent the gospel spreading to all the nations.

WHAT IS HAPPENING IN HEAVEN DURING THE THOUSAND YEARS (REVELATION 20:4-6)

Revelation 20:1-3 describes what is happening on earth during the thousand years. Verses 4-6 describes what is happening in heaven during this time.

In first-century Rome, persecutions raged. Christians were thrown to the flames and to the wild beasts in Roman amphitheatres. The Lord Jesus was not unmindful of them and wanted to encourage and sustain them. He did this by giving them a vision of the souls in heaven. He wanted them to know that the persecution and hostility they were facing would be worth it in the end.

These people who suffered real persecution for the testimony of Jesus (1:2, 9; 6:9), in some cases even being beheaded, are now seated on thrones and reigning with Christ. This should encourage Christians today who may be suffering for the cause of Christ.

At the moment, during this thousand-year period, it is their souls and not their bodies that reign. It is only when Christ returns to this world and the final judgement takes place that these souls in heaven will have new bodies.

It is not only the martyrs who are with Christ, but all those who have died trusting in him. This should really excite us. If we trust in Jesus Christ, the moment we die our souls go to be with him. Two thieves were crucified at the same time as Jesus, on crosses either side of him. They were bad men and deserved the punishment they were getting. One of them repented at the very end and was sorry for all that he had done. He asked Jesus to remember him. Jesus said to him these breathtaking words, 'Today you will be with me in paradise' (Luke 23:43). The moment a person who is trusting in Jesus Christ dies, their soul goes straight to be with him in paradise.

THE FINAL CONFLICT (REVELATION 20:7-10)

When the thousand years are finished, Satan is unchained and released from prison. During this short period, sometimes referred to as 'Satan's little season', there will be a terrible persecution of the church. Satan will gather Gog and Magog for battle and they will march the breadth of the earth and surround the camp of God's people.

The expression Gog and Magog is borrowed from Ezekiel 38. It refers to the terrible persecution of God's people under Antiochus Epiphanes, ruler of Syria. The book of Revelation uses this period of affliction and woe as a symbol of the final attack of Satan against the church. There are many resemblances between the terrible persecution under Antiochus Epiphanes and what will happen at the end.

Firstly, the attack of Gog and Magog was the last great oppression which the people of God had to endure in the old dispensation;

whereas 'Satan's little season' will be the final conflict the church will ever have to face. Secondly, the armies of Gog and Magog were very numerous, symbolizing worldwide oppression of the church at the end. Thirdly, the oppression under Antiochus Epiphanes, though very severe, was also a very brief duration. In the same way, even though 'Satan's little season' will be terrible, it will be very brief. Fourthly, the defeat of the armies of Syria was unexpected and complete; it was totally the work of God. Similarly, at the end, Jesus will come suddenly and his victory over the devil and the forces of evil will be complete.

It is also important to keep in mind that the battle described in Revelation 20:7-10 is the same battle as in Revelation 16:12ff and Revelation 19:19ff. It is the battle of Armageddon, the final attack of antichristian forces upon the church. During this time, Satan deceives the world into thinking Christ can be defeated. Maybe you are thinking like this. Maybe you think that the Bible cannot really be true. There cannot really be a heaven and a hell. Jesus Christ isn't really coming back to judge the world. Be careful, because suddenly Christ will come and conquer all who oppose him (cf. 2 Thessalonians 2:8).

At this time the devil will be cast into the lake of fire and brimstone. Even though their punishment has already been described, he actually goes down at the same time as the beast of the earth and the beast of the sea and the people who bear the mark of the beast, which is everyone who rejects Jesus Christ.

Make sure you are not among that number, that vast number, whom the devil will succeed in deceiving!

THE GREAT WHITE THRONE (20:11-15)

When the Lord Jesus Christ does return to this world to defeat Satan, his helpers and all his followers, he will sit on a great white throne. All the dead, great and small, will stand before this throne.

Imagine it! Every great historical figure will stand before this throne. Every king, queen and world leader that has ever lived will stand before this throne. Film stars, pop stars, sports men and women will stand before this throne. Tramps, beggars, 'ordinary' people, Asians, Americans, Europeans, Africans, 'good people', terrorists, rapists, murderers, will all stand before this throne. You and I will stand before this throne.

As we are standing there, the books will be opened and the record of the life of every person will be read out. The book of life containing the names of all believers will also be opened.

Imagine two different people on that day. They both stand before this great white throne and everything in their lives has been recorded.

The one person's turn will come and God will say, 'Review his life.' It will start from when he was a baby, 'for there is nothing hidden which will not be revealed' (Mark 4:22, NKJV). It will show him as a teenager and then as a man. He will have to give an account of every word he has spoken (Matthew 12:36). Every impure or lustful thought he has had will be shown (Matthew 5:28). 'For there is nothing covered that will not be revealed, and hidden that will not be known' (Matthew 10:26, NKJV). This person has heard the gospel and has been offered Jesus Christ as his Saviour but he rejected him because he wasn't interested. He was too busy. The cost was too great and he didn't want to give up his sin. As he stands before this great white throne, he realizes he must have been insane and it dawns upon him that it's all too late and he's guilty and without Christ and damned for ever! God commands the book of life to be opened and an angel says, 'His name does not appear, Lord.' Then he hears the most chilling words anybody will ever hear, 'Depart from me, you cursed, into the everlasting fire prepared for the devil and his angels' (Matthew 25:41, NKJV). And he will go away into everlasting punishment (Matthew 25:46). Visualise it! Imagine it! Sent to hell for ever!

Now consider the other person. Just as much a sinner as the first one; but he repented of his sin and put his trust in the Lord Jesus Christ. He would say, 'For to me, to live is Christ and to die is gain' (Philippians 1:21, NKJV). As he stands before this great white throne he has nothing to answer for, because Jesus Christ has taken all his sin and guilt and clothed him with his own righteousness. He stands before this great throne as if he's never done a thing wrong. More than that, he stands before that throne as if he was as good as Christ himself! He's got nothing to fear. The book of life is opened and his name is found. It is unimaginable, the eternal, never-ending joy he is about to enter. 'As it is written; eye has not seen, nor ear heard, nor have entered into the heart of man, the things which God has prepared for those that love him' (1 Corinthians 2:9, NKJV).

Maybe you are a Christian reading this book and are worried about standing before this great throne. But if you are trusting in Jesus Christ you have nothing to fear. You will stand before it clothed in his righteousness as if you've done nothing wrong.

I taught a boy whose father was a bit of a small-time crook. He and his mate once broke into a factory and stole a load of materials. They were caught red-handed. However, they managed to get themselves a hot-shot lawyer. They went to court and stood in the dock and the lawyer made the case for their defence. He said that there was no way that his clients could have been in the factory on that particular night and no way they could have taken the materials they were accused of taking. His case was so powerful and convincing that the boy's father turned to his mate and said, 'Perhaps we didn't do it'!

On judgement day, when everyone will stand before this great white throne, Christians will have someone far greater pleading their eternal cause for them. The elect will turn to each other and say, 'It's as if we didn't do it.'

In his famous hymn, Zinzendorf says,

> Jesus, Thy blood and righteousness
> My beauty are, my glorious dress.
> Midst flaming worlds, in these arrayed
> With joy shall I lift up my head.
>
> Bold shall I stand in that great day
> For who aught to my charge shall lay?
> Fully absolved through Thee I am
> From sin and fear, from guilt and shame.

However, if you are not trusting Jesus Christ, you have no idea of how terrifying it will be to stand before that great throne alone. Come to the Saviour now while he will still receive you.

19

THE NEW HEAVEN
AND THE NEW EARTH

Revelation 21:1-8

THE NEW HEAVEN AND THE NEW EARTH (21:1-8)

The previous chapters have recorded the defeat of all the enemies of the Lord Jesus Christ. In Revelation 15 and 16 we saw what would happen to the people who bear the mark of the beast, that is, everyone who rejects Jesus Christ. In chapters 17 - 19 we were shown the destruction of the prostitute Babylon (godless society), the beast of the sea (antichristian persecution) and the beast of the earth (false religion and philosophy). In chapter 20 we saw the defeat of the one behind it all, the dragon, Satan. All evil, wickedness and sin have been defeated and now in Revelation 21 and 22 everything is made new (21:5).

At the beginning of chapter 21 John sees a new heaven and a new earth, for the first heaven and the first earth had passed away

(21:1). This is so certain of happening that in verse 6 the one who sits on the throne says, 'It is done'.

It is not just human beings who are under the sentence of death, but the whole of creation. The way things are today is not the way they are supposed to be. The entire creation groans and suffers, waiting for all things to be made new. One day this tormented, distressed, afflicted earth will be wrapped up and there will be a new heaven and a new earth.

In this new order God will dwell with his people (21:3). Christians will enjoy God's company for ever. We cannot really imagine what it will be like. It takes us to the limits of our imagination.

No more sadness

Every tear will be wiped away and there will be no more death, or mourning or crying or pain (21:4). The world we live in knows so much heartache and sadness — illness, bereavement, relationships breaking up, issues with ourselves, issues with other people, the way we look, depression, family problems, financial worries, failure. We all know something of these in one way or another. Mr Higham often said, 'He has not travelled far who has no wound or scar.' But one day all things will be made new and there will be no sadness at all.

No more sea

There will also no longer be any sea (21:1). In chapter 13 the beast comes out of the sea. In Isaiah 57:20 the wicked are compared to the tossing sea which cannot rest, whose waves cast up mire and mud. There is no peace. The sea stands for chaos, death and destruction; but in the new heaven and the new earth there will be no more sea.

The spring of the water of life

Those who are thirsty are able to drink from the spring of the water of life without cost (21:6). The spring of the water of life is heaven. It is eternal life and it's free! Maybe you are trying to earn your own salvation, trying to save yourself. You turn over a new leaf, stop doing certain things, give up bad habits, read your Bible, pray, attend church. Stop trying to earn your salvation! You cannot make yourself right with God. Only God can make a person right with God. For a long time John Bunyan, the author of *Pilgrim's Progress*, prayed, 'Forgive me for my sins, I'll try harder tomorrow.' But after a while he realized, 'I can't be any better; please save me.' Come and drink of this water of life freely!

The ones who inherit eternal life are the ones who have overcome (20:7). These are the ones who stood against all the persecution and were not deceived by the false religion and thinking of this world. They were not seduced by the prostitute Babylon; and even though they were pursued by the dragon they overcame him by the blood of the Lamb.

The lake of burning sulphur

But the cowardly (spineless in the face of persecution), the unbelieving, the vile, the murderers, the sexually immoral, those who practise magic arts, the idolaters and all liars will be banished to the fiery lake of burning sulphur (21:8).

Here is a warning that all sinners who will not repent and turn away from their sin will spend an eternity in hell. Maybe you think that this seems very cruel and that you don't really feel you are bad enough to spend eternity in such a terrifying place. But every one of us is contaminated with sin. Through circumstances or temperament or background we may hide it better than others; or we may not have had the opportunities to sin as much as we could have. But every one of us has a sinful heart. Given free rein and left to our own devices we are capable of the worst of sins. According to a report printed in the *Journal of the American Institute of Criminal Law and Criminology* 18, no. 1 (May 1927),

> *Every baby starts life as a little savage. He is completely selfish and self-centred. He wants what he wants when he wants it: his bottle, his mother's attention, his playmate's toys, his uncle's watch, or whatever. Deny him these and he seethes with rage and aggressiveness which would be murderous were he not so helpless. He's dirty, he has no morals, no knowledge, no developed skills. This means that all children, not just certain children but all children, are born delinquent. If permitted to continue in their self-centred world of infancy, given free rein to their impulsive actions to satisfy each want, every child would grow up a criminal, a thief, a killer, a rapist*
>
> (From the *Minnesota Crime Commission Report of 1926*, commissioned by then Governor Theodore Christianson).

God takes sin seriously. It has to be dealt with, either on the cross of Jesus Christ or in hell for all eternity. I urge you to come to the Saviour now before it is too late.

In his poem, Bertram Shaddock describes the petrifying scene on judgement day for all those outside of Jesus Christ:

> *I dreamed the great judgement morning had dawned and the trumpet had blown,*
> *I dreamed that the nations had gathered for judgement before the white throne,*
> *From the throne came a bright shining angel who stood on the land and the sea*

*And swore with his hand raised to heaven, time was no longer
 to be;*
*And oh what a weeping and wailing as the lost were told of
 their fate,*
*They cried for the rocks and the mountains, they prayed but
 their prayer was too late.*

Make sure that when time ends and there is a new heaven and a
new earth that you are dwelling with God and not in the fiery lake
of burning sulphur.

20

THE NEW JERUSALEM

Revelation 21:9 - 22:5

In attempting to explain the meaning and symbolism of Revelation 21:9 - 22:5 I feel completely inadequate and out of my depth. It is very difficult to try to portray the wonders of what John saw because I do not really understand and appreciate these things myself, let alone try to explain them to others. They are magnificent and beyond description. I am too sinful and don't know God well enough to do justice to them. With that in mind let us proceed to look in some way at what John saw.

In Revelation 21:9-10 John is carried away in the Spirit to a great and high mountain, where he was shown a city coming down from heaven. The city is described in Revelation 21:9 - 22:5. It is called the New Jerusalem because Jerusalem was the city of God in the Old Testament (Psalm 46:4). The temple was in Jerusalem and the place signified God's presence.

The city is huge. It extends fourteen hundred miles in each of its three dimensions. The city is a perfect cube and is made of gold.

The walls of the city are great and high. They are 144 cubits, which is about 65 metres, thick. The city is built on twelve huge, precious, foundation stones. The colour of each foundation stone is different; red sardius, white jasper (diamond), blue sapphire, green emerald and so on. The city has twelve gates: three on the east side, three on the south side, three on the west side and three on the north side. Each gate is a huge pearl and is a doorway to a street or avenue. These streets or avenues are made of pure gold. Alongside these avenues are rivers of the waters of life which flow from the throne of God and of the Lamb. Between the streets on the one side and the rivers on the other side there are trees which bear an abundance of fruit every month of the year. The leaves of the trees are able to heal the nations. What a city!

The city is a description of the church. It is not a description of heaven. It is showing what the church, the people of God, will be like one day. All these symbols apply in principle now, but we will enjoy them in perfection in the future. That the city is the church is clear from the way John mixes his metaphors. In Revelation 21:9 the angel says to John that he will show him the bride and then takes him away to a high mountain to show him a city (21:10). The bride and the city are one and the same. As we know from Revelation 19 and other parts of the Bible, the bride is a description of the church; and so this city is a description of what the church will be like one day.

Some people are a bit disappointed when they realize that it is a description of the church and not of heaven. However, we shouldn't be. Heaven will be at least as beautiful as the city described in Revelation.

But here, in Revelation 21 and 22 we have a description of the people of God, the church, which makes what John saw even more wonderful. People are so much more important than places and buildings and gates and streets and so on. Every year I go on holiday to Cornwall with my wife and little boy. We stay in a cottage and it is the highlight of our year. There's no place like Cornwall to us; Truro, St Ives, Padstow, Crantock. We love it. But the reason we really love it is because the three of us are there together. With anyone else it wouldn't be the same. The people make it special. What is so wonderful about this city in Revelation 21 and 22 is that it is a description of God's people and at the centre of this city is God himself! Heaven will be wonderful for so many reasons; but primarily because we will be with God and enjoying his presence in the company of all his people, for ever.

In order to help us appreciate how wonderful the church will be, let us look at some of the details more closely.

The city (21:10-11, 16, 18)

The city is huge. It extends fourteen hundred miles in length, breadth and height. That is roughly the distance from London to Moscow. It shows that when all the people of God have been gathered in at the end of time they will be more than any man can number. Maybe you attend a small congregation on a Sunday and find it hard and feel a bit alone. You may attend conferences or camps every year and love being with other Christians and are sad to leave and go back to your little congregation on a Sunday. Keep in mind, one day you will be part of this great, eternal city. You will be in the presence of God's people for ever, never to have to leave them.

The city was made of gold, which shows it is precious and beautiful. We are shown here what God really thinks of the church. In his eyes the church is beautiful and precious. Think about how the church appears to other people today; how others esteem her. Think about the condition of the churches in chapters 2 and 3 of Revelation. They were pitiable small groups persecuted by mighty foes. Today the church in some parts of the world is persecuted; in other places the church is made fun of and seen as old-fashioned, out-of-date and ridiculous. What the church has to say is completely unimportant to the overwhelming majority of twenty-first-century people. But to Almighty God, the creator of heaven and earth, the one who sits on the throne of the whole universe and whom angels bow down to and worship, she is beautiful and precious!

A couple had been married for many years and the wife was taken ill with cancer. In the latter stages of the illness, the cancer had ravaged her body. As she was approaching death the husband took the minister to see her in hospital. By this time she looked dreadful and was completely disfigured. As they stood by her hospital bed, the husband turned to the minister and said, 'Isn't she beautiful?'

Even today, in the state we're in, God looks at the church and says, 'Isn't she beautiful?' But what is even better is that one day she will be made beautiful and precious. The church will no longer split and have divisions; no longer will the people of God gossip and hurt one another; no longer will we fall into sin and be plagued by it. We will be beautiful. The city will shine with the glory of God and its brilliance will be like that of a very precious jewel (21:11).

The walls of the city (21:12, 17-18)

The walls of the city were great and high, and 144 cubits (about 65 metres) thick. Not only is this city precious and beautiful; it is also secure and safe. Nothing now can harm the people of God. No more threat of persecution; no more being plagued by our past and troubled by our consciences; no more doubts; no more worries about the future. Safe for ever!

What is not in the city (21:22-27)

John saw no temple. In the Old Testament the temple was the meeting place between God and sinners. God's presence was in the temple. Today there is no need for people to go to the temple to have fellowship with God. In John 4 Jesus Christ told a Samaritan woman that there would come a day when people would not need to go to the temple because God could be worshipped anywhere. We live in those days today. We can pray to God anywhere, anytime and sometimes we can know him draw very near to us, especially in times of revival. But in the future we will be in God's immediate presence all the time. That is why in the city that John saw, the Lord God Almighty and the Lamb are its temple.

There was no sun or moon because God gives this city light and the Lamb is its lamp. There will be no more night and no shadows at all. Nothing to be scared of. Everything will be light and good and clean. There will be no impurity of any kind.

The foundations of the city (21:14, 19-20)

There were twelve foundation stones, each one a precious stone. John stood and watched this city come down from heaven. Inscribed in these stones were the names of the twelve apostles. Imagine what John would have thought when he saw this awesome city come down from heaven and on one of the stones he saw his own name, John.

The meaning of these foundation stones is clear: the foundation of the church is the teaching of the apostles, the Word of God. The Bible is the foundation on which the church is built. The Bible is the Christian's sole authority for what he believes and how he is to live. All teaching must be tested by what the Bible says. The Word of God is more important than the traditions of the church, our own human reason and any feelings or leadings we may have. According to Dr Lloyd-Jones:

> *The church is built upon the foundation of the apostles and prophets. We must therefore reject every supposed new revelation, every addition to doctrine. We must assert that all teaching and all truth and all doctrine must be tested in the light of the Scriptures. We can build only upon this one, unique, authority*
>
> (Quoted in Jeffery, *Christian Handbook*, p.21).

This city is built on the beautiful truths and laws of God's Word. It will be wonderful to dwell for ever in a city built upon these foundations: no stealing, lying, murder, hate, infidelity, gossip, jealousy and pride, but only kindness, justice and goodness.

The gates of the city (21:12-13, 21, 25)

There are twelve gates: three on the east, three on the south, three on the west and three on the north. On each gate was written one of the names of the twelve tribes of Israel. Each gate was a pearl. Pearls are precious. Jesus told a story of a man who sold all that he had to buy a pearl of great price. This pearl symbolized the gospel and shows it is worth giving up everything else to obtain.

When a person becomes a Christian they give up their old way of life and turn from their sin and put their faith in Jesus Christ. Every Christian will tell you it's worth it, like entering pearly gates. This is seen in the life of Martin Luther. He was desperate to be right with God. He tried all sorts of things in his attempt to have peace with God. One day as he read Romans 1:17 he realized that to have all his sins forgiven and to have eternal life in heaven he simply had to put his faith in the Lord Jesus Christ. As this dawned on him he said it was like the gateway to paradise.

The names of the twelve tribes of Israel on the gates, along with the names of the twelve apostles on the foundation stones, represent the entire people of God. That there are gates on the east, south, west and north of the city shows that God's people will come from all over the world and that everyone is welcome. The open gates show that everyone can have easy access to this city from all four corners of the world. Today you can enter this city.

Furthermore, people shut gates and lock doors at night; but there will be no more night. There is nothing to shut out; security measures are no longer necessary. There is no evil or harm to be concerned about.

The streets of the city (21:21)

Every gate is the door to a street and the city is full of beautiful streets made of pure gold. These streets all lead to rivers and trees of life.

The city centre (22:1-5)

At the centre or heart of this city is the throne of God. Flowing from this throne are the rivers of the water of life. By these rivers are trees which produce an abundance of fruit every month of the year. These images should be taken together and show the abundance of our salvation, everlasting life and our fellowship and communion with God.

Think of all the people of God. They will make up a great crowd with many needs and desires and yet there are trees and fruit and rivers in abundance. There will be more than enough for everyone.

All the people of God will one day enjoy intimate fellowship and communion with Christ for ever. Whatever Christ has, we have;

wherever Christ is, there we will be too. This is seen several times in the book of Revelation. In Revelation 14:1 Christ is pictured standing on Mount Zion and with him are all his people. In Revelation 19:11 heaven is opened and the Lord Jesus Christ comes forth on a white horse and in Revelation 19:14 his people were all following him on white horses. In Revelation 3:21 the Lord Jesus says that he will grant all his people the right to sit with him on his throne.

The leaves of the trees heal the nations. Eternal life heals all misery and sin. Think about all the suffering that is in the world today. All the heartache, illness and pain. Family breakdown, unhappy childhoods, broken promises, shattered dreams. Pasts that haunt us. One day we will know complete healing from all these things.

Above all, Revelation 22:4 says that one day we will see his face. I can't really imagine standing face to face with the Lord Jesus Christ knowing that before the sun, moon and stars were put in their places he loved me; that 2000 years ago on that little hill outside the city of Jerusalem he died for me; that he's seen everything I've done, knows everything I've thought and heard everything I've said and yet I am still a member of this great city. When I see him face to face, all I'll be able to say is, 'I can't believe you loved me and gave yourself for me!'

There is no greater privilege than being part of this city. John Newton put it like this in one of his hymns:

> Saviour, if of Zion's city
> I through grace a member am,
> Let the world deride or pity,
> I will glory in Thy name:
> Fading is the worldling's pleasure,
> All his boasted pomp and show;

Solid joys and lasting treasure
None but Zion's children know.

It is impossible to fully grasp how amazing the church will be one day. It is beyond our comprehension to imagine the splendour of heaven she will enjoy. The eighteenth-century Welsh hymn-writer, William Williams, thought heaven was too far away to see clearly.

The lenses lack the power, the distance is too vast.
I comprehend but dimly the glorious life to last.

Just make sure that through faith you are a member of this city; because, as Paul says, 'No eye has seen, no ear has heard, no mind has conceived what God has prepared for those who love him' (1 Corinthians 2:9, NIV).

CONCLUSION — JESUS IS COMING!

Revelation 22:6-21

In the conclusion of the book, John stresses the importance of Revelation. It's important because Jesus is coming! In the light of this, he gives us serious warnings and amazing promises.

Don't add to or take away anything from Revelation

Nobody must add to or take away anything from this book (22:18-19). This is a real warning to so-called Christians who add their own traditions to the Bible and give the same authority to the words of a man as they do to the Word of God. It is also a warning to those who deny or try to change parts of the Bible. Anyone who tampers with this book will not share the tree of life (have eternal life) and will suffer the plagues that are described in this book. The one who keeps the words of the prophecy is blessed, favoured by God (22:7).

The urgency of Revelation

John is told not to seal up the words of the prophecy of this book (22:10). God wants everyone to read it. The message of the book could not be more important. Today people spend their time emailing, texting and tweeting online 'friends' about such effluvium as what they ate for lunch, in ever more abbreviated language. Neal Gabler in the *Los Angeles Times* (*The Week*, 11 December 2010) described the future as 'one in which words are abundant but exist mainly to express the trivial and the transitory'. Revelation is far from trivial and transitory and so much more important and exciting than a message from an online 'friend'. It is from Almighty God and its message has eternal consequences. Heaven and hell are at stake.

What is more, it is an urgent message because the end is near (22:10). The Lord Jesus Christ says in verse 12: 'Behold [take note], because I am coming quickly'; and again in verse 20: 'I am coming quickly'. It could not be clearer nor emphasized more. Make sure you are ready because Jesus Christ is coming back!

Imagine being on an aeroplane where one of the passengers is wearing a parachute. You'd think he was odd and a bit over the top — until you found out that he had been told the plane was going to crash suddenly during the flight. Even though he might be a bit uncomfortable and look a bit silly, you'd think he was doing the right thing in being prepared. Everyone else who did not want to die would reach for the nearest parachute. Maybe you think that people who put their trust in Jesus Christ and follow him are mad and over the top. But if this book is true and its message is real then surely the only thing to do is reach out in faith and put on Jesus Christ.

All people who do not repent of their sins and do not reach out and take hold of Jesus Christ will be lost for ever (22:15).

The good news of Revelation

Revelation 22:14 says, 'Blessed are those who wash their robes for they will enter the city.' The people here are pictured as once having filthy robes which were stained by sin. But they have come to Jesus Christ to have their robes washed in his precious blood. All who come to Jesus Christ can have their sins washed away and all their guilt removed. Whatever you've done, whatever you've been trying to hide, his blood can make the foulest sinner clean. The hymn-writer Elisha Albright Hoffman asks us:

> When the Bridegroom cometh, will your robes be white,
> Pure and white in the blood of the Lamb?
> Will your soul be ready for the mansions bright
> And be washed in the blood of the Lamb?

Then he tells us to:

> Lay aside the garments that are stained with sin
> And be washed in the blood of the Lamb;
> There's a fountain flowing for the soul unclean;
> O be washed in the blood of the Lamb!

In Genesis 3:24, after Adam and Eve sinned, the whole of humanity was prevented from approaching the tree of life. But now, through the blood of Jesus Christ, they have perfect freedom to come to the tree of life. What is more, now there is no chance that those who enter the city will ever be thrown out. Jesus Christ secured more than Adam lost. As Kistemaker says, they have 'never-ending residency' (*Revelation*, p.590). No wonder the church longs for Christ to come (22:17, 20)!

CONCLUSION

Don't play around with the God of Revelation

Revelation 22:11 (NASB) says, 'Let the one who does wrong, still do wrong; and the one who is filthy, still be filthy.' The use of the word 'let' here is negative. It's as if the Lord Jesus Christ is saying, 'If they want to sin, let them be. Leave them to carry on.' God pleads with sinners to repent; but there comes a point when he leaves them to their own devices. No one knows when God's patience will run out with them and he will harden their heart. If you've heard the voice of Jesus pleading with your heart, come to him; because he may stop pleading and instead say, 'Let him be.'

So what will you do with this Revelation?

At the centre of the book of Revelation is a person, the God-Man, the Lamb, Jesus Christ. You cannot be passive or indifferent towards him. You either accept him or reject him. One day you will stand before God and he will ask you: 'What did you do with him?' How will you answer on that awesome day?

There is a famous nineteenth-century painting by Ciseri called 'Ecce Homo'. The painting, which hangs in the Palazzo Pitti Gallery in Florence, is based on Jesus' trial before Pilate. It takes its title from Pilate's words to the crowd: 'Behold the man!' or in Latin, 'Ecce Homo!' In the painting, Jesus stands on the terrace, stripped to the waist, his hands bound behind him. Pilate stands in the middle of the painting, with his back to the viewer. He is leaning forward, head bent over the railing, appealing to the masses gathered below him in the streets. With one hand he gestures toward Jesus, as if to ask: 'What will you do with him?'

It is the most important question you will ever answer. Your eternal destiny hangs on it!

APPENDIX

APPROACHES TO
AND BASIS FOR INTERPRETING REVELATION

APPROACHES TO REVELATION

There are four main approaches to the book of Revelation.

The first is known as the 'preterist' approach. Those who hold this view believe that the author is describing in symbolic form what took place in his own time. The events refer to the time of the persecuted church which is parallel to the period of Revelation being written. This approach confines our understanding of Revelation to that particular time, the first century. It tends to make the book of Revelation an interesting historical commentary on the church in the first century but does not have much relevance to the twenty-first-century church. By itself this approach does not seem helpful to the church today.

The second is known as the 'futurist' approach to Revelation. This approach is concerned with the future and sees the book of Revelation as interpreting events at the end of the world. It is all about the end of time and relates exclusively to the last days. This approach would not have helped the churches in Asia in the first century in their situation. All it would have to say to the church at that time is that there is a hope at the end of time.

The third is known as the 'historicist' approach to Revelation. This approach views Revelation as a chart of world history from the first coming of Christ right up to his second coming and the entry of his people into glory. The seven churches are not seven churches in Asia but refer to seven eras in the history of the church. One of the problems with this approach is that those who propose it cannot agree on what historical events and periods the book is referring to. It can be very subjective.

The fourth is known as the 'idealist' approach to Revelation. This approach maintains that Revelation simply deals with principles which are always valid in the church's experience. This approach does not secure Revelation in an historical setting or period.

As far as this writer can see, elements are necessary from all four approaches to understand Revelation. There is not one solitary approach to Revelation but a fusion of all four approaches. According to Mounce:

> *The author himself could without contradiction be preterist, historicist, futurist and idealist. He wrote out of his own immediate situation, his prophecies would have a historical fulfilment, he anticipated a future consummation, and he revealed principles that operated beneath the course of history* (*Revelation*, p.29).

For a proper understanding of the book of Revelation we must start with the people to whom the book was first addressed. This is a basic principle in interpreting any book in the Bible. The people to whom the book was first written were a persecuted people. They had put their faith in Jesus Christ and then almost immediately had to face the venom of an antichristian society poured out against them. They saw what seemed to be the dismantling of the Christian church and wondered who was in control. Revelation wasn't a puzzle book but a letter addressed to seven particular churches to help them and show them that God was on the throne and that there was another dimension to reality.

However, Revelation isn't just a letter and it doesn't only speak to the Christians in the first century. John saw the Roman Empire as the great beast that threatened the extinction of the church; but the particular beast that John saw isn't just the Roman Empire but all 'beasts' that oppose the church.

Revelation deals with what will happen and is happening throughout history from Christ's first coming right up until his second coming and into eternity. In this way Revelation is prophetic and apocalyptic.

APOCALYPTIC

Revelation has been identified as a type of apocalypse. Apocalyptic literature was popular among Jews and began to appear in the third century BC as a response to persecution. The authors of apocalypses claimed to be passing on heavenly mysteries revealed to them by an angel or some other spiritual being and the writers usually used extensive symbolism. Apocalypse is always eschatological (teaching about the last days) and strongly contrasts this world with the world to come.

Revelation possesses many of the features described and there are many good reasons to support the classification of Revelation as apocalyptic with its symbolism, visions and teaching on the end times.

However, there are differences between Revelation and apocalyptic writings. Apocalypses are typically pseudonymous, whereas the author of Revelation, John, writes in his own name. Furthermore, Jewish apocalyptists grounded their hope in a future event, while John in Revelation grounds his hope in the past; the death and resurrection of Jesus Christ, 'the Lamb that has been slain'. Apocalyptic writing also tends to be pessimistic. Although there will be an outbreak of satanic activity and the church will suffer persecution, history remains under the control of God and a genuine and real optimism permeates the whole of the book of Revelation. Revelation is therefore best described as 'an apocalypse with a difference' (Carson, Moo and Morris, *An Introduction to the New Testament*, p.479).

PRE-, POST- AND AMILLENNIALISM

The word millennium means one thousand years. Revelation 20:4-5 (NIV) says that certain people 'came to life and reigned with Christ for a thousand years. (The rest of the dead did not come to life until the thousand years were ended.)' Revelation 20:1-3 says that an angel came down from heaven and seized the devil, bound him, threw him into the pit, and shut it and sealed it over him so that he should be unable to deceive the nations for a thousand years.

Throughout the history of the church there have been three major views on the time and nature of this 'millennium'. Some of the church's greatest Bible teachers have held different views on the meaning of the thousand years and have therefore interpreted the book of Revelation in different ways.

Postmillennialism

According to this view the progress of the gospel and the growth of the church will gradually increase, so that the world's population will become more Christian. As a result, there will be significant Christian influences on society and gradually a millennial age (which isn't necessarily a literal thousand years) of peace and righteousness will occur on earth. At the end of this period Christ will return to this earth, believers and unbelievers will be raised, the final judgement will occur and there will be a new heaven and a new earth and everyone will then enter the eternal state.

This whole idea, however, does not seem to fit in with what the Bible tells us respecting the great apostasy towards the end of time (Matthew 24:9-13, 21, 22) — though some postmillenialists do believe that there will be an apostasy at the end of the millennium.

Premillennialism

According to this viewpoint, as the world nears the end, a time of great tribulation and suffering comes to the earth, after which Christ will return to earth to establish a millennial kingdom. When he comes back, believers who have died will be raised from the dead and their bodies will be reunited with their spirits. These believers will reign on earth for one thousand years with Christ, who will be physically present on earth in his resurrected body. The believers who have been raised from the dead and those who were on earth when Christ returns will receive glorified resurrected bodies that will never die. At the beginning of this time Satan will be bound and cast into the bottomless pit so that he will have no influence on the earth during the millennium (Revelation 20:1-7) and so there will be peace throughout the earth. Many of the unbelievers who remain on earth at this time will turn to Christ and be saved. Some premillenialists believe that the new heaven and new earth will be ushered in at this time.

At the end of the thousand years Satan will be loosed from the bottomless pit and will join forces with many unbelievers who have submitted outwardly to Christ's reign but inwardly been seething in rebellion against him. Satan will gather these rebellious people for battle against Christ, but they will be decisively defeated. Christ will then raise from the dead all the unbelievers who have died throughout history and they will stand before him for final judgement. After the final judgement has occurred, believers will enter the eternal state.

Some premillenniallists are also dispensationalists. They hold to the premillennial view but add to it a secret return of Christ before he returns to the earth to reign for a thousand years. This return will be sudden and unexpected and believers will be taken out of the world (1 Thessalonians 4:16-17). Christ will then return to heaven with those believers and there will follow a period of tribulation that will last for seven years. During this time many Jews will turn to Christ and despite great tribulation it will be a period of effective evangelism.

At the end of the tribulation Christ will return to earth and reign for a thousand years and so on.

It seems to this writer that the premillennial approach is based on a literalistic interpretation of the prophets and of Revelation 20:1-6. However, this passage makes no mention of the Jews, of an earthly and national kingdom, or of the land of Palestine as the place where Jesus will rule. Furthermore, the rest of the New Testament knows nothing of such an earthly and temporal kingdom of Christ.

Amillennialism

According to this position Revelation 20:1-10 describes the thousand years as being symbolic of world history between Christ's first and second coming. The thousand years are not to be taken literally, but are symbolic of a long period of time. Just before Christ's second coming there will be widespread apostasy, that is, a turning away from the Lord Jesus Christ and opposition to the gospel, which will reach its climax in the appearance of the Antichrist. The Lord Jesus Christ will suddenly return to this world and conquer Satan and the forces of evil and will judge all people. On this day, the dead will be resurrected and they too will be judged.

Even though great men have adopted post- and premillennial interpretations of Revelation, this writer holds to an amillennial approach.

SYMBOLISM

Revelation is a book full of symbols. We are not to take these symbols literally but try to find out what they mean. In order to do this the writer of this book has tried to interpret these symbols against the background of the conditions which prevailed when the book of Revelation was first written. Also, the writer has interpreted them in the light of similar imagery and symbols in the Old Testament and the New Testament, holding firmly to the belief that the best way to interpret and understand the Bible is to compare Scripture with Scripture.

BIBLIOGRAPHY

Barnes, S. *The Meaning of Sport* (London: Short Books, 2007)

Blanchard, J. *Evolution: Fact or Fiction?* (Darlington: Evangelical Press, 2003)

Bunyan, J. *Pilgrim's Progress* (Edinburgh: Banner of Truth Trust, 1997)

Carson, D. A., Moo, J. and Morris, L. *An Introduction to the New Testament* (Leicester: Apollos, 1993)

Christofides, A. *The Life Sentence* (Carlisle: Paternoster, 2002)

Dallimore, A. *George Whitefield: The life and times of the great evangelist of the 18th century revival*, volume 1 (Edinburgh: Banner of Truth Trust, 2001)

Dawkins, R. *The God Delusion* (London: Black Swan, 2007)

Edwards, B. *Revival — a people saturated with God* (Darlington: Evangelical Press, 2004)

Fox, J. (ed. Forbush, W. B.) *Foxe's Book of Martyrs* (Grand Rapids: Zondervan, 1978)

Grier, W. J. *The Momentous Event* (London: Banner of Truth Trust, 1970)

Henry, M. *Matthew Henry's Commentary on the Whole Bible Complete and Unabridged* (Peabody, Massachusetts: Hendrickson, 1995)

Hendriksen, W. *More Than Conquerors* (Grand Rapids: Baker Books, 2006)

Houghton, S. M. *Sketches From Church History* (Edinburgh: Banner of Truth Trust, 1991)

James, L. *The Rise and Fall of the British Empire* (London: Abacus, 1998)

Jeffery, P. *Christian Handbook* (Bryntirion: Evangelical Press of Wales, 1988)

Kistemaker, S. J. *New Testament Commentary: Revelation* (Grand Rapids: Baker Academic, 2007)

Lambert, T. *China's Christian Millions* (Sevenoaks: OMF, 2006)

Leahy, F. S. *Great Conversions* (Belfast: Ambassador, 1999)

Lenski, R. C. H. *The Interpretation of St. John's Revelation* (Minnesota: Augsburg, 1943)

Lewis, C. S. *The Screwtape Letters* (London: Fount Paperbacks, 1992)

Lloyd-Jones, D. M. *The Church and the Last Things* (London: Hodder and Stoughton, 2002)

Maier, P. *Josephus: The Essential Writings* (Grand Rapids: Kregel, 1988)

Morris, L. *Tyndale New Testament Commentaries: Revelation* (Leicester: IVP, 2009)

Mounce, R. H. *The New International Commentary on the New Testament: The Book of Revelation* [revised edition] (Grand Rapids: Eerdmans, 1997)

Packer, J. I. *Concise Theology* (Leicester: IVP, 1993)

Plummer, A. *The Book of Revelation* (Pulpit Commentary) (Grand Rapids: Eerdmans, 1950)

Tozer, A. W. *The Pursuit of God* (Carlisle: OM Publishing, 1993)

Wilson, G. B. *Revelation* (Welwyn: Evangelical Press, 1985)

Young, E. *The Complaint: or, Night-Thoughts on Life, Death and Immortality* (Hartford: S. Andrus and Son, 1847)